Seeing Christ in Others

Geoffrey Duncan was for many years the Information officer
of the Council for World Mission, the affiliating body for
churches in the reformed tradition around the world – a
position he held until early in 1998. He has now the
opportunity to become a full-time writer and editor. He is the
compiler of *Dare to Dream* published by Fount. He is married
to Pat and lives in North London.

Seeing Christ in Others

Compiled and edited
by
Geoffrey Duncan

CANTERBURY
PRESS

Norwich

First published in 1998 by The Canterbury Press Norwich
(a publishing imprint of Hymns Ancient & Modern Limited,
a registered charity)
St Mary's Works, St Mary's Plain,
Norwich, Norfolk NR3 3BH

British Library Cataloguing in Publication Data

A catalogue record for this book is available
from the British Library

ISBN 1-85311-192-9

*Typeset in Great Britain by Rowland Phototypesetting Limited,
Bury St Edmunds, Suffolk
Printed in Great Britain by Biddles Limited,
Guildford and King's Lynn*

To Pat, Jane and Ruth

You each practise love in your own different ways and for this I am grateful – you teach me so much.

Contents

Foreword

Long before the Internet was even a twinkle in its inventor's eye, there was an invisible network of communication linking people across the world through what I believe to be the telepathic power of prayer. In this book, Geoffrey Duncan helps us to 'surf that net' by enabling us to listen to and share in the prayers of people from many parts of the world.

An anthology of prayers is rather like a collection of letters, written in different circumstances and attempting to express varied human experiences – of love and joy, of pain and regret, of confession and sympathy. I often find it as difficult to find the right words to express myself in prayer as I do to write a letter. So I am always grateful for the help I can get from others who have tried to express the same longings, who have struggled to find the right words, and whose prayers I can make my own. There are many prayers like that to be found in this volume.

What impresses me is the wide compass of sources from which these prayers have been drawn. As one who has travelled the world myself, I have often been given new spiritual insights as I have heard the prayers of people from different cultures, but sharing our common needs. I wish I had taken as much care as Geoffrey Duncan has done to record and preserve such prayers to share with a wider constituency. He has put us all in his debt by producing such an ecumenical and international collection for us to use.

In a newspaper article a few months ago, Archbishop Desmond Tutu was asked how he explained the miracle that happened in South Africa, where such momentous change had been brought about without the appalling blood bath that so many people feared. His answer was characteristically brief and blunt. 'We've been prayed for, you see,' he told the interviewer, 'and by heck, man, it works, it really works!' One of the most effective ways of praying for people is to pray *with* them, and I am so glad that Geoffrey Duncan has included in this anthology prayers that remind us of our inter-relatedness as we pray with people on the other side of our world – quite literally so, for several of the prayers come from Australia and New Zealand.

This is a book which will be useful not only in private devotions but also to those of us called to lead public worship. It is always important to remind local congregations that they never come to worship as an isolated community but as part of that world wide fellowship, whose prayers were being offered long before our own day of worship began and whose prayers will continue to ascend long after our day is over. A book like this can help to make real to people the fact that 'the voice of prayer is never silent'.

Pauline Webb
October, 1997

Introduction

People talk . . . dream . . . dance . . . sing . . . go on retreat . . .
seek silence . . . meditate . . . pray . . . break bread together . . .
search for new ways of knowing Christ . . . seek release for
marginalised companions . . . for prisoners . . . the list is endless. People search for ways in which their dreams can become
reality; how their dreams can become positive actions which
are earthed in community and take root as they look for Christ
in others.

One of my dreams, very soon after *Dare to Dream* was published and the first excitement receded over the horizon, was
to compile a second anthology. It was with great delight that I
accepted the invitation to compile *Seeing Christ in Others*.
There are four sections, Searching and Seeing, Listening and
Loving, Serving and Setting Free and Glimpsing the Kingdom.
There is a natural progression within the flow of the book
although, as ever, material can be used contextually from
any section for private devotions and corporate worship.
Searching and Seeing enables us to search for and see Christ in
the midst of our ordinary, everyday lives. When we become
aware of humankind – all the many and different people – we
will meet our living Christ and find the unexpected church in
our societies. By our Listening and Loving we shall meet our
compassionate Christ in our neighbours especially when we
listen to the hurting people in our communities. Regardless of
the labels which are attached to human beings; rich, poor,
marginalised, indigenous, all these companions are people in
their own right. Everyone needs a listening, loving person
alongside them.

When we search, not too deeply, and when we listen and love we shall be Serving and Setting Free people who are oppressed. New ways of service will open and people will be set free. In cities, rural areas, remote villages, deserts, by the oceans of the world, in our homes, schools, aboriginal settlements, townships, women's development centres, half-empty or half-full churches, there are people, each one of whom is precious. Through these companions whether they are working, worshipping, relaxing or finding space we shall be Glimpsing the Kingdom in many different ways. Search, Love, Serve, see Christ in others! It may not be easy but each person will be involved in their own particular way so continue your journey with encouragement and enthusiasm.

Many people have provided items to help me compile *Seeing Christ in Others*. I am very grateful to new friends and acquaintances from around the world and to friends from earlier years who have written new material or given me permission to use work already in existence. Sincere thanks to my wife Pat, Joy Button and Isabel Hathaway who have given their services and valuable advice voluntarily as they searched journals from around the world, sorted papers, compiled the index, listed copyright permissions and kept smiling when I surrounded them with piles of paper. Also, I am appreciative of the support given me by Christine Smith, my publisher at The Canterbury Press. Christine has been a source of strength and always offered advice and encouragement at the right time.

Let us all keep in touch, writers and readers, as I believe there is a worldwide network of people who can support each other as we continue to see Christ in other people. Until next time, Shalom.

Geoffrey Duncan
October 1997

Searching and Seeing

Christ in Me, Christ in Others

Christ, take my emptiness;
    may it be a space for you.
        And may I encounter you
           in everyone I meet.

William Rutherford
Northern Ireland

The Everywhere Christ

(To be used in worship with one or two voices or as a congregational response)

Through human lips
Christ is speaking
Through human hands
Christ is healing
Through our hearts
Christ is loving
Through us all
Christ is working
So behold the truth
God is living, loving
speaking and healing
through Christ our Saviour.

Richard Becher
England

Waiting for My Lord

I sat all day
in the shade of the banyan tree,
turning my face
to the distant hills and waited

3

for my Lord to come.
My heart pounded heavily
with expectation
and my eyes burned.
The morning passed away
and the noon melted
into evening and the evening
into darkness.
But he did not come.

I recalled that a poor mother
and her child passed by that way,
then an old man with a bundle of
firewood and later
a traveller who lost his way.
I hardly even looked at them.
At the fall of night
I went into my hut
and lay awake on my bed
with a heavy heart
and then I heard a voice
saying:
'I passed by you thrice
but you did not see me.'

Solomon Raj
India

The Silent Cry

Does anyone care
that I sit and stare
and wonder why
I'm here at all?

A still small voice
whispers – Yes – Rejoice
You're a precious stone
in my Kingdom's wall.

Harry Wiggett
South Africa

Pilgrim People

Jesus said: 'If anyone wants to come with me, he must
forget self, carry his cross, and follow me.
For whoever wants to save his own life will
lose it:
but whoever loses his life for me and for the
gospel will save it.'

The people of God have always been pilgrims, called to follow
him with only the promise that he will be with them. No
assurance that life will be comfortable and secure. No agreement that there will be no hard times, confrontations, periods
of uncertainty. Rather the reverse.

And the people of God suffer and give up the struggle ...
suffer and become resigned to suffering ...
suffer but still sing for joy.

Being a pilgrim means having no abiding city.
Being a pilgrim means following rough, overgrown paths and
winding through narrow alleyways as well as striding along
the main street.
Being a pilgrim means trying to companion other pilgrims
who have strangers' faces and who speak unfamiliar
languages.

Being a pilgrim is to accept all that Jesus means when he says
'Follow me' ... a total willingness to let go of the past, fulfil the
present and welcome the future in order to proclaim the
gospel of the living God.

Jill Jenkins
England

Features

The gnarled and lined features of an East End immigrant
The black tragic face of a Rwandan refugee
The anguished tearful gaze of a Bosnian widow
The scarred features of a tortured South American priest;
in all of them I see the thorn-crowned face of Christ.

John Johansen-Berg
England

Hospitality

I asked Love to help me
greet the stranger in myself.
I knew how to open my door to the world
and greet everyone out there as friend
but I didn't have any kind of welcome
for the impoverished one within.
She was the weakness I couldn't acknowledge.
She was the pain I didn't allow.
She was the leper I'd tried to cast out the city,
the one who cried at night in lonely places.
I thought that if I let her in
she'd cause me no end of trouble,
and I was afraid.

But Love helped me to prepare a feast.
We set the table, Love and I,
and then I did it,
I invited my stranger.

6

'Answer the door,' said Love.
'You have nothing to fear.'

She came in slowly.
I put my arms around her
and embraced her in her rags
and we wept together for years of separation.
I sat my stranger at the head of the table,
gave her the best of food and wine
and, claiming her as my own,
began to introduce her to my friends.
'But who shall I say she is?'
I whispered to Love.
'I can't call her a stranger now.'
Love smiled and said, 'Don't you know?
She is the Christ.'

Joy Cowley
Aotearoa New Zealand

Because You Came

Because you came and sat beside us,
because you came and heard us speak,
and we ignored you and we refused you,
    we ask forgiveness, Lord Jesus Christ

Because you laughed and loved the child-like,
because you lived from day to day,
and we love status and steady money,
    we ask forgiveness, Lord Jesus Christ

Because our peace was your agenda,
because you wept to see us at war,
and we love power and winning battles,
    we ask forgiveness, Lord Jesus Christ

Because your Cross compels an answer,
because your love absorbs our sin
and we are wounded because we wound you,
    we ask forgiveness, Lord Jesus Christ

Because you came on Easter morning,
because you come at Pentecost,
and in the Spirit, we are forgiven,
    we live to praise you, Lord Jesus Christ!

Shirley Erena Murray
Aotearoa New Zealand

Jesus Today

Where would you walk today, Jesus?
Would you enter our inner cities triumphantly,
surrounded by the homeless, the lost and unloved?
Would they cheer you or jeer and beg?
Maybe even mug you and leave you for dead
    like the man on the road to Jericho.

Where would you walk today, Jesus?
Would you walk through our leafy suburbs looking
    for the crowds to listen?
People shut behind neat windows, neighbour
    ignoring neighbour.
Quiet streets, empty lives.

Where would you walk today, Jesus?
Would you sit in our churches, half empty, half full?
Would you lead us in worship; would we listen to you?
Our Sabbath no longer special with all the days the same?

Would we share your vigil in Gethsemane, Jesus?
Would we care, would we keep vigil with you,
Or would we sleep, watch television or just simply forget?

Would we crucify you again today, Jesus?
When a child is unloved or abused, the old,
    ignored and unwanted,
the poor, homeless and needy everywhere,
We crucify you again and again.

Where are you today, Jesus?
Where do we look?
Where people love you Jesus; love others as well,
Where people give themselves in caring for others,
Where faith gives hope and hope brings love
that is where we see you Jesus, today.

Jill Denison
England

The Human Touch

It need not be the money
one gives to charity
but the heart that gives the penny
with humanity.

It need not be the smiles
one scatters full and plenty
but something really worthwhile
to cheer a life that's empty.

It need not be the handshake
to show one's friendliness
but in the time of heartbreak
a touch of kindliness.

One does not have to shower
words of honeyed speech
but in a needy hour
a word a heart to reach.

The human touch is unique
it is something from within
it gives one's deeds a finish
is sure the words you mean.

Alice Saldanha
India

The Busker

You play your tune.
Crowds surge past.
Most give nothing,
not even a glance.
You have the attention
of a few pavement people:
a youth with a skinny dog
who always sits in that doorway,
a woman with her life in paper bags.

Christ the busker,
I've got your tune in my head
but head music is not enough.
Help me to be a busker too.

Janet Lees
England

God Be with Those Who Explore

God be with those who explore in the cause
of understanding; whose search takes them
far from what is familiar and comfortable
and leads them into danger or terrifying
loneliness. Let us try to understand their
sometimes strange or difficult ways; their
confronting or unusual language; the
uncommon life of their emotions, for they
have been affected and shaped and changed

by their struggle at the frontiers of a wild
darkness, just as we may be affected,
shaped and changed by the insights they
bring back to us. Bless them with strength
and peace.

Michael Leunig
Australia

I Searched for You in Dusty Libraries

I searched for you in dusty libraries,
in old manuscripts and daring new texts
but I did not find you.
I searched for you in banks
and in busy building societies with eager customers
but I did not find you.
I searched for you in gilded cathedrals
and in decorated basilicas with crowds of tourists
but I did not find you.

I visited the shanty town of Mathare Valley,
saw the basic tin and cardboard huts
and heard the story from the women
who bring initiative and new hope into this bleak situation.
I met with villagers on remote Palestinian hills
and saw them building terraces to retain the soil
and make the desert blossom and bear fruit.

I spoke with refugees from Rwanda and Burundi
and met with pastors committed to a ministry of
    reconciliation
in spite of danger and hostility.
There I found you,
Christ of the poor, living with the hungry and oppressed,
inspiring the work for justice and for peace.

John Johansen-Berg
England

Don't Hide

Don't hide:
don't run,
but rather
discover in the midst of fragmentation
a new way forward:
a different kind of journey
marked by its fragility,
uncertainty
and lack of definition.
And on that path
to hold these hands
that even in their brokenness
create a new tomorrow.
To dance at the margins,
and to see
the face of Christ
where hurt
is real and
pain a way of life.
To be touched
in the eye of the storm,
aware that tomorrow
may not bring peace.
Impossible, you say;
let me retreat
and find my rest.
What rest, my friend,
in these fragmented times?

Peter Millar
Scotland

In Prayer

In prayer I feel so small,
a speck of dust

and you Lord
of the Universe
stretched out
beyond me and underneath,
a reality so firm and huge.

In prayer I feel in place
hidden but nevertheless
part of things
watching your
love unfold,
colouring the
landscape.

In prayer I see the hands
of Christ reach over
and out to the world
and hold the
pieces together,

and I am there
somewhere.

Valerie Shedden
England

Jesus Says

If your ears are for hearing,
  then listen carefully.
If your eyes are for seeing,
  then look upon me.

Do not look among the clouds –
  the birds are there already.
Do not search ocean deeps –
  the fish have preceded you.

Follow me along the road
　　and you will find yourself.
Know me on the journey
　　and you will know yourself.

If you do not know yourself,
　　everything is poverty,
but if the light is within you,
　　the whole world shines.

Carve the wood or help the stranger
　　and you will find me.
Shape the stone or tend the sick
　　and I will be there.

Bruce D. Prewer
Australia

Walk Among Us Jesus

Look at the world, look at each other
　　see the pain and see the tears;
　　see the face of Jesus.
Wounded people, angry people;
　　hungry people and thirsty people,
　　we see broken people everywhere.
We see them, we hear them;
　　shouting and crying,
　　brothers and sisters together
　　in the one family of God

Walk among us Jesus,
walk among us now
so the world may see you
revealed through our lives.
(Response between the verses)

Walk on the battlefield,
    talk to the soldiers,
    reconcile the leaders
    and console the mourning families
    as you reveal yourself to us today
    for the world to see your peace.

Walk our city streets,
    talking to the lost,
    healing the broken hearted
    and giving new hope
    as you reveal yourself through us
    so the world may know your presence.

Walk in our darkness
    with a light to show the way,
    forgiving hardened hearts,
    reaching those rejected
    and giving strength in weakness
    as you reveal yourself through us today,
    so the world can see your love.

Walk into our churches,
    opening locked doors
    so people may find you
    know you and hear you
    and lift up your cross
    to follow you out
    so the world may know
    the truth you have revealed.

Richard Becher
England

To Live Is To Go Around –
Leaving Bits of One's Own Life

Ay bendito, Jesus, we need a clear understanding of what we must do in order to come to grips with the reality of our time. The everyday experience leads us to the cross to be borne by each life, in each situation, in each place.

Lord, when your cross is planted firmly on the ground it points to the infinite, and it becomes a meeting point between the depths and the heights. There the splendour of your purity mixes with the superficial nature of human relations. There the fences built up against human understanding are broken down, and humankind can learn to forgive. There a new style of communication is opened up, unveiling your relation to God. Other than for the fact of the cross (which we are definitely bearing), who could believe any of this today, Jesus? Today Ebenezer* is no longer a point of reference on the road. Emmanuel offers consolation to the afflicted, stimulus to the intrepid, and reward to the generous.

To live now means to go around leaving bits of one's life among those who are being crucified daily in the midst of a suffering people. Living today is also being aware of your presence, Jesus, in every human being, in every circumstance. Each hut is a sanctuary of your presence and signifies an invitation to accompany you and to lend you a hand. Each human being is a witness to your grace, and each new day a hope that begins to take shape to the rhythm of your mercy. Along the roads and paths of this life the builders of the new humanity traverse, reasserting the validity of your word, which the forces of evil insist on drowning out.

Along those paths we are going, Jesus, walking under the shadow of your cross, which itself continues to represent madness and a stumbling block to the unbelieving and spiritually stingy. For us it is a prophet signal announcing the coming of the kingdom of justice and peace. And we can already discern the glorious day when you will reconcile, unite, renew, and reinstate those of your children who await your coming while working at concrete tasks.

In the meantime, we'll see each other around, Lord, on the road.

* 1 Samuel 4:1

Juan Marcos Rivera
Puerto Rico

To Be Fully Human

To be fully human, fully myself,
To accept all that I am, all that you envision,
This is my prayer.
Walk with me out to the rim of life,
Beyond security.
Take me to the exquisite edge of courage
And release me to become.

Sue Monk Kidd
England

God of Good Ideas

God of good ideas,
who began the world
with light and word,
who began again
with flood and rainbow;

We acknowledge our frustration with your church:
its committees and structures,
its methods and systems.
These things have made us angry and sapped our energy.

17

God of new beginnings
    who began a new way
    of living with resurrection,
    who began a new community
    with tongues of fire;
    begin again here
    that structures may bend
    like dancing saplings;
    that past, present and future
    may be woven into
    a fresh path of commitment.

May our ideas for your world and this community
    resonate in your presence,
    so that tested, tried and challenged
    they may blossom in us
    as do dry places
    when longed-for rain falls.

Janet Lees
England

Search

    Is He really here in this vaulted place,
    Or is it simply a vacant space
    Carefully created in crafted stone –
    An empty tomb,
    Discarded womb
    Of an age-old story of camels and kings,
    Of angels and shepherds, and shining star,
    Told to persuade you of who you are?

    Is He really here in this cloistered place?
    No, He is the life-light in your face –
    You bring Him with you when you come
    Within your heart –
    Essential part

Of the ebb and flow of the essence of you –
Of sorrow and joy, of wisdom and pain ...
Of His Spirit within revealed again.

So seek Him not in this ancient place,
But see Him in each other's face –
His star reflected in every eye ...
He comes with you
In all you do –
In your love of the drunk upon the floor,
Of the war-torn child, of the sick and the poor –

For the age-old story was true.

Margot Arthurton
England

God in Hiding

God in hiding, we will seek you;
we will cross the thorny ground,
where you sit among the shadows,
playmate longing to be found;
we will risk ourselves with Jesus,
learn from him hope's searching ways,
follow him through deepest darkness,
dare with him, life's tangled maze.

Jesus searched the dark before us,
grieving in Gethsemane;
crossing death's abyss to find you
through the gloom of Calvary.
You were calling from the darkness,
urging him to brave love's night;
you were waiting to receive him
in your resurrecting light.

Still your Spirit, hiding in us,
urges us to seek and know
your persistent, wounded presence
where we hardly dare to go.
Though earth's sorrow overwhelm us,
as we long to see your face,
we will love you in our neighbours,
find, with them, your hiding place.

Alan Gaunt
England

God Gathers

As a workman gathers his tools,
as a poet gathers her images,
as a musician gathers his band,
as a scholar gathers her arguments,
as a writer gathers his stories,
as a preacher gathers her texts,

so God gathers people for service.

Stephen Brown
England

Living with Contradiction

Lord this life is full of contradiction,
I myself am an embodiment of that contradiction
In that my life is characterised by:
Both love and hatred,
Strengths and weaknesses,
Light and darkness,
Sorrow and joy,
Humiliation and upliftment,
Truth and falsehood,
Direction and chaos,
Self and others,

Life and death.
All these are weighing so heavily on me,
Yet you, God of heaven who knows all these,
Have decided that you will use me
In your world, for your purposes.
Help me then:
To see myself,
To see others,
    and
To see this life with your eyes.

Rupert Hambira
Botswana

I Hold the Loving Cup

I hold the loving cup, full to overflowing,
ready to drink but waiting –
waiting for a companion to drink with me.
There are plenty of cups of poison,
and fellow travellers ready to share the cup of hate.
But who will drink with me from the cup of love?
I search in the killing fields of Rwanda;
I walk along the walls of Derry, looking;
I journey through the shattered villages of Bosnia.
Who will drink together of the cup of love?

John Johansen-Berg
England

Journeying

Often when taking our own journey
we find ourselves in a cul-de-sac,
or at a crossroads not knowing which road to go
or on a roundabout where we circle endlessly.
Journeying with others we find the way

as we go on with purpose, guided by the divine Spirit,
towards a common goal.

John Johansen-Berg
England

Christ Our Advocate

Christ our advocate,
we pray for our sisters and brothers throughout the world:
    out of our poverty and theirs,
    may we not stumble
    by judging each other.

Christ, brother of the poor,
in the faces of our partners may we see your love.
    In our faces may they see your love.
    Together may we abide in you,
    celebrating the risen life of the Kingdom.

Christ, bridge-builder,
help us to work with you and for you.
    Through the power of the Spirit
    help us to rebuild God's community of divine purpose
    in partnership with all your people.

Kate McIlhagga
England

Teach Us

O God,
the delicate balance of your creation
is slowly being stripped of its riches:

    your streams of living water
    are choked with chemicals;
    your life-giving trees
    droop and die;

Open our eyes to see, and our ears to hear
the cry of your creation.
Teach us its wonders.
Teach us to cherish and protect your world,
Teach us how to live in partnership
with all things,
that we may learn how to live
as one body in Christ –
   dependent on each other's gifts,
   sharing in each other's hopes.

Kate McIlhagga
England

It Rained Most of the Night

It rained most of the night and the next morning was another driving-wet day. The rain was sweeping against umbrella'd figures, sending them scuttling into doorways or burying themselves in cars.

He went to the restaurant he had been in every day, wondering why there was no sign of the young man and the girl. Nearing the end of his stay, there he sat, doing nothing. Looking out to sea, yes, but with nothing really to look at. Only one ship was passing, way off in the distance, hard to see. It was moving away from him.

The rain eased a little then came on again, as hard as ever, midday, as soon as he had left the restaurant. He shared his umbrella with a chap in a parka as they stood under some trees.

'I'm wet through as it is,' the young man muttered, 'what with going up to the hospital. I was asking after that bloke as knocked himself out. That dishy piece in the sunhat was with him. You must have seen her. He was jumping off the seawall, showing off, just as I'd have done if I'd had the chance. They say he'll be okay.'

'That was good of you.'

'Well, she really is quite something ... and quite cut up about him. Thanked me for going along.'

When the rain eased off a bit, he saw people stepping out from behind tree after tree, people he had never dreamed were anywhere near. Countless throngs of them, they kept coming into his line of vision, and he had thought there were just the two of them there, under their shared umbrella, mid-way through the trees, whilst all the time there were all these people (lot of drips like himself) ... (drip, drip, dripping), under the trees.

He followed his new-found friend as he passed through the midst of them.

Brian Louis Pearce
England

Café

A damp night of it; no window
keeps out the widower's wind.
The flame spits, dies on the hearth.

Rain rails. Devils billow
black against glass of the mind,
wash out lit sticks. The path

up to the café's shook door
swills with water. The cell
sunk in the park like a pit

in Jerusalem fit for
drowned Jeremiah, swells
and entombs. Lightning's hit

24

what's left of the café two mock-
ers had burnt to a char for a bet.
Yet a damp pair were buoyed

there tonight by some bloke who broke
the bread the three of them ate:
he must have come in from the void.

Brian Louis Pearce
England

God of Surprises

God of surprises, startle us
with truth we do not see,
amaze us with your power and grace,
awaken us to be
your thankful children, minds attuned
to your eternal mirth
expressed through that first cry for life
we utter at our birth.

Great God of mystery, beckon us,
and lead us far above
restricted hope and narrow faith
to demonstrate your love.
Then, as we strive to serve you here
in true humility,
fulfil creation's dream of joy
in vibrant harmony.

Moira Rose
England

The Noise Nothing Makes

It's funny how my mind chooses to speak
    the words of my heart
when the busyness of life stops and my ears

YORK
R.E.
CENTRE

grow accustomed to the noises of others
　　whilst I sit quietly basking in the
nothingness that suddenly surrounds me.

A void filled to the brim with desires and hopes
　　yet to be discovered,
desires that have not yet formed into thought,
　　word or vision.

　　Hopes that confront me face on
when I look into the wanting eyes of those who
　　see myself as
　　Hope Personified.

Little do they know that hope will never
　　cease to exist.
　　She is everywhere

wherever the lost souls float hopelessly
　　in the nothingness
　　Hoping, Seeking, Looking
　　for fulfilment.

Feiloaigia Taule'ale'ausumai
Aotearoa New Zealand

Palm Sunday

No donkey this time
but a borrowed Honda 550.
Jesus riding into town
with a black leather jacket,
jeans frayed at the knees,
and L-O-V-E tattooed
on the knuckles of his right hand.
Those who saw him
said his smile was like the sun,
warming shadowed corners

and causing the way to blossom
unexpectedly.
Those who saw him told
of all the light left over
to be taken home and set
in eyes, in hearts
and at windows for strangers.
It was like a miracle,
they said.

The rest of us missed it.
We were in another part of the city,
waiting for the Messiah.

Joy Cowley
Aotearoa New Zealand

Holy Saturday

In that room there was light
struggling with darkness
and birthing hope from despair.
A family gathered in a communion
that needed no bread or wine
to speak of minds and bodies broken.

Love reached beyond the outward appearance
accepting a loved one
as he was
because of what had been
and what might yet be.

No turning away, here, to ease the pain,
but reality faced and challenged
by a refusal to capitulate
to superficial definitions of worth.
Here significance is discovered in care
given and received.

I saw the Holy Christ
resting in that bed,
as in the tomb,
through love which values all,
God turns the place where hope is dead
into an Easter waiting room.

Peter Trow
England

In a World of In-between

Like shorebirds living between sand and surf
we live in a world of in-between

between punching the clock and smelling the roses
   serving others and renewing ourselves
between hanging on and letting go
   sticking with the old and risking the new
between speaking truth and sparing feelings
   seeking justice and avoiding division
between the economy and the environment
   the 'loonie' and the loon
between computer byte and human touch
   avoiding harassment and needing a hug
between who we are and what others think we should be
   who we are and who we may become

We are shorebirds living
between cross and rolled away stone
between the alpha and the omega
   the beginning and the end

And the spirit of the one
who walked the shore before us
walks with us
hallows this in-between world
as God's world —

We are not alone
Thanks be to God

Norm S.D. Esdon
Canada

Shame

Lord, you said you would come.
In your love you give us a world;
a vibrant, living, pulsating world.
And to our shame we poison it.
Come and cleanse hearts.

In your joy you give us companions,
to care, enrich and learn from each other.
And to our shame we do not listen.
Come and open ears.

In your compassion you give us yourself,
walking, talking, revealing your love.
And to our shame we ignore you.
Come and wash eyes.

We nail your mouth shut, but still you come,
with arms open wide to embrace us all,
every land of your creation.
And we wait for you.

Lord, come for your land,
and in your mercy,
hear our prayer.

Duncan Tuck
England

No Harm Meant?

(Towards more inclusive language)

I meant
unhappy
You heard
BLACK
Pig-ment

I meant
all people
You heard
MEN
Debase-ment

I meant
... but equal
You heard
NO CHOICE
Debar-ment

I meant
Discuss
You heard
OBEY
Impedi-ment

I meant
I'm sorry
You heard
NO – WAIT
Resent-ment

I meant
I'm wrong
You heard

YOU'RE RIGHT
Atone-ment?

Edward Cox
England

Make Us a Prejudiced People

Lord God,
make us a prejudiced people:
passionate
to pursue your loving justice;
passionately opposed
to all that obscures the hope
and destroys the purpose
and denies the reconciliation
that is your will for us.

Lord God,
make us a prejudiced people:
ready to speak up for
all that is good and true in your sight;
ready to speak out against
all that is an abomination to your eyes.

Lord God,
make us a prejudiced people:
turned to
the light of Christ;
turned from
the darkness of our own misdeeds.

Lord God,
make us a prejudiced people:
united
to seek to do and to bear your will;
divided

from all that distracts us from being the
people you intend.

Stephen Brown
England

We Are Caught in a Dragnet

We are caught in a dragnet deep beneath the sea;
you and I struggle for survival;
around us are some of our own kind
and others of a hundred different breeds.
What have we in common
as the dragnet draws us closer together?
A longing for help and
an inward conviction that all will be revealed,
all separated and sorted.
Our hope is in our maker not in ourselves.
We have learned that his name is love,
so we reach out to each other
as the net draws us ever closer.

John Johansen-Berg
England

An Advent Call to Worship

Come from your homes
With Christmas cards unwritten
With family arrangements yet to be finalised
Come share in a celebration
Which began with the homeless, the illiterate
    and the unmarried.

Come from your places of work
With 'To-Do' lists as long as your arm
With in-trays overflowing and phone calls put off
    yet again
Come share in a celebration

Where our work is to worship and our ceremony
   is to set us free.

Come from your communities
Where talk is of Christmas shopping
And where our children are whipped up by
   advertising frenzy
Come share in a celebration
Where we have nothing to peddle but our
   stories of hope.

Come from your nations
Where immigrants are unwelcome
And politicians vie for your vote
Come share in a celebration
Where the proud will be scattered and the
   rich sent away empty.

Come Holy Spirit
Come Father and Mother of new life
Come let us worship
Come let us turn our lives upside down.

Edward Cox
England

Advent Feet

God, your advent feet come silently
along our noisy streets;
the noise, our ears, the silence
contain the Christ we FAIL to greet.

God, your advent feet come silently
along our noisy streets;
the noise, our ears, the silence
contain the Christ we FEAR to greet.

God, your advent feet come silently
along our noisy streets;
the noise, our ears, the silence
contain the Christ we LONG to greet.

E. Body
Aotearoa New Zealand

Were We There?

If only we'd known
As we crowded into the inn that night,
Pushing and shoving to get our places!
We were determined not to be left out in the cold,
So we arrived early.

The innkeeper and his wife were harassed
As they packed us in,
Squeezing our blankets into the smallest space,
Rushing us from the tables
To feed the following crowd.

How good it was to rest
After that wearying journey.
The Romans didn't care
How much it cost us to get there,
Either in terms of money, or of time.
What did it matter to them
That we'd had to travel the length of the country?
Did they assume
We'd all stayed in the birthplace of our fathers?
So when we arrived
We were glad to find a place
And so concerned with our own welfare,
We had no time for others.
The inn was warm,
The food was good,

We met old friends,
The wine flowed freely
And we were only thankful
It was not us that the innkeeper had to put into the stable
Because the inn was full.

We did not sleep well that night.
There were too many people
In too little space
And the smells and sounds were incredible!
But we heard nothing outside.
We saw no lights in the sky,
Heard no sounds from the stable,
Except the animals
And a far-off baby's cry,
which was nothing to what we heard inside the inn!

So, next morning we left,
Packing our bags and paying the bill
And glad to get out into the air again
to finish our journey,
Register our names
And turn around to face the road to home.
If only we'd known!

But how could we?
Bethlehem seemed the same that night
As any other.
And we were not aware
There had even been a birth!

Marjorie Dobson
England

Nativity

Look now!
It is happening again!
Love like a high spring tide
is swelling to fullness and overflowing
the banks of our small concerns.

And here again is the star,
that white flame of truth
blazing the way for us
through a desert of tired words.

Once more comes the music,
angel song that lifts our hearts
and tunes our ears
to the harmony of the universe,
making us wonder how
we ever could have forgotten.

And now the magi within us
gathers up gifts of gold and myrrh,
while that other part of ourselves,
the impulsive, reckless shepherd,
runs helter skelter with arms outstretched
to embrace the wonder of it all.

We have no words
to contain our praise.
We ache with awe,
we tremble with miracle,
as once again,
in the small rough stable of our lives,
Christ is born.

Joy Cowley
Aotearoa New Zealand

Faith

Strange elusive certainty
Of those who seem to know
The way they face,
Whose Revelation comes in simultaneous step
With fate's demands,
And, effortless, completes
The rounding off
Of all events.
What gift is theirs,
What surety of aim,
Acceptance, acquiescence ...
This universal answer
To a never-stated question ...
This absolute acknowledgement ...
This strange elusive certainty –
This Faith.

Margot Arthurton
England

Burned Church

There has been sorrow here –
And loss –
And fiercely funnelled flame
Fuelled by rage here ...
There has been burning here –
Savage, wanton, swift,
To brand the place
With smouldering desolation.

There has been darkness here.
And broken beams here,
And fractured dreams.
And charred remains ...

There has been ash here,
And water, steam, and acrid smell,
And overall and pall
Of hell here ...

But the stone still stands –
Like rock on rock
The House is built ...
The sky looks down upon the place,
And in the sun, revealed,
The previous face of all renewal
Smiles.
For in a little while
The day will surely come
When ash and dust are lost
In time's eclipse,
And sorrow fades –
For in the husk of grief
There lies a seed
Which waits in secret quiet
Upon the ripening of the time –
Whose fullness will fill full
The empty space,
And thus fulfil with shining face
The aching need.

Margot Arthurton
England

Fallen Angels

Can we aspire to walk upon the water,
Or feed a milling crowd on little bread
When we ourselves conspire in death and slaughter
And worry only that our own are fed?

What right have we to judge the acts of others
And, sanctimonious, talk of God above –

When, surreptitiously, we cheat our brothers
And disillusion most the ones we love?

So do we really think that we are better
Because we weekly go and sing in Church –
And know the prayers precisely to the letter
And say we have no further need to search?

How can we pander to such vain illusion,
And think, in arrogance, that we are right –
When, shrouded darkly in its own confusion,
Humanity eclipses its own light.

Margot Arthurton
England

What You Do to the Least

It was my first trip to the beautiful city of Kyoto, Japan. My
host had sent the necessary information for me to reach him in
Kitayama. In Kyoto I looked for the subway for the last lap of
my journey but failed miserably to locate it. As I stood in the
middle of nowhere with local people staring at me, an old man
walking feebly approached me with a kind of smile. He
inquired about my problem. Soon, both of us discovered that
we could not speak each other's language. I showed him a
piece of paper which carried the name and telephone number
of my host, but no address. The old man assisted me to the
information booth and as we walked I noticed that he had
great difficulty in walking due to a disability. The problem
became even more difficult at the booth but somehow I was
able to convince one of the officers to try and telephone my
host. Thank God, my host was still at home but about to leave.
Like a defeated explorer I asked him to speak with the old
man. With the sound of a familiar language it took no time for
the old man to understand the problem. Holding my hand
tight he took me through the splendid subway shopping arena
of Kyoto station to the underground station. The subway

mystery was solved but the story continued. At the entrance he did not let me buy a train ticket as he had a special escort ticket which was free on account of his disability.

Sometimes silence expresses emotions far better than words. Sitting next to him as the train to Kitayama made its journey I tried to express my deep gratitude and thankfulness, knowing full well that in spite of all his limitations he had the will and compassion to help a stranger like me.

On sighting my host at the destination I ran to greet him and turned back to introduce the good samaritan. He was making his way through the other exit, bowing traditionally and waving at us with a big smile.

Harold Williams
India

Prayer for Peace

Show us, good Lord,
　　the peace we should seek,
　　the peace we must give,
　　the peace we can keep,
　　the peace we must forgo,
　　and the peace you have given in Jesus our Lord.
　　And in reconciling man to man and man to God.
Help us, as individuals or together,
　　to work, in love, for peace, and never to lose heart.
We commit ourselves to each other
– in joy and sorrow;
We commit ourselves to all who share in the
　　work of reconciliation
– to support and stand by them.
We commit ourselves to the way of peace
– in thought and deed.

We commit ourselves to you
– as our friend and brother.

Author Unknown

A Mother's Prayer

Lord you are in my baby's awakening
Your Spirit is filling her
Your Spirit is Peace

Lord you are in this playful washing
Your Spirit splashed her
Your Spirit is Peace

Lord you are in the way I feed her
Your Spirit satisfies her
Your Spirit is Peace

Lord you are in the games I play with her
Your Spirit delights in her
Your Spirit is Peace

Lord you are in the song I sing to her
Your Spirit soothes her
Your Spirit is Peace

Lord you are in her time of sleep
Your Spirit keeps her
Your Spirit is Peace

Bob Commin
South Africa

The Garden

Come and plant a garden
    by scattering the seeds of love
    and watching peace grow.

Then scatter the seeds of peace
    and harvest the fruits of justice.
Then scatter the seeds of justice
    and witness the flowering hope.
And when you scatter the seeds of hope
    you will walk in the garden of paradise.

Richard Becher
England

May the Blessing of Light

May the blessing of light be on you,
light without and light within.
May the blessed sunlight shine upon you
and warm your heart
till it glows like a great fire
and strangers may warm themselves
as well as friends.

And may the light shine out of the eyes of you,
like a candle set in the window of a house,
bidding the wanderer to come in
out of the storm.

May the blessing of rain be on you;
the soft sweet rain.
May it fall upon your spirit
so that little flowers may spring up
and shred their sweetness on the air.

And may the blessing of the great rains be upon you,
to beat upon your spirit and wash it fair and clean;
and leave there many a shining pool
where the blue of heaven shines,
and sometimes a star.

May the blessing of the earth be upon you,
the great round earth;
may you ever have a kindly greeting for people
as you're going along the roads.

And now may the Lord bless you,
and bless you kindly.

An Irish Blessing

By the Lake of Galilee

Jesus watched the fishermen at work,
waiting to call them to follow him.
He heard the gentle sound of the sea
beneath the shadow of the boats,
washing over the sand
and drawing out again,
the constant change of the tide,
rising and falling,
shifting and cleansing the sand,
bringing into the shore the warmth of the sun
and reflecting its light and power
in the changing pattern of waves and ripples.

The ministry the disciples would share with him
would be like that, always moving, bringing change
to the lives of people and communities,
making them new.

He watched the sun set,
beautiful and splendid,
thinking of darkness that brings fear,
doubt and pain before dawn comes;
of people hungering and thirsting for righteousness,
struggling for freedom from pain and injustice:
sunset is the promise of another day.

Life was never the same again for the fishermen.
When waves and clouds hid the sun,
now and then they caught reflections
of light in the storm
and knew that God was present –
with them –
restlessly seeking, and changing the world,
to restore harmony to every part of creation.

Maureen Edwards
England

The Stranger

Why were people so angry with Jesus
that day when he preached
in the synagogue at Nazareth?
Why did they attempt to kill him?
Was it because he dared to say
he saw a sign of God's presence
in the action of a poor widow
of another race?
It was not the righteous people of God
but the stranger.
And he saw God's presence
in the unbelieving Naaman,
a Syrian,
who recognised the true prophet
and asked to be healed.

In Christ, God broke into life,
coming from the outside,
a stranger.

Strangers are rarely welcome:
they see too clearly
our empty respectable ways,
our insularity

and the chains of our religion.
They side with outcasts
and offend the good and worthy.

They are always present,
coming in from the streets,
the developing world,
from prison,
poorly dressed and hungry,
piercing our ignorance
with insights
from their own bitter experience.

Maureen Edwards
England

Faithful People

I am lost. I stop and look around. Granite boulders tower to my left and right. They look familiar. Acacia trees spread their branches over the grassland in between. They look familiar but where is Zompata church? The half-finished brick building should be in front of me. Nothing. Where are the people? My basket of bread, communion cups, juice and books becomes heavy. With a sigh I turn back and retrace my steps to the truck, climb into the cab and wait. Half an hour later, just as I am thinking about leaving, a church member appears.

'Pastor,' he says, 'you are here!'

'Am I happy to see you! I came looking for you but I got lost. I am so glad you've come.'

'Next time you will know the way,' the church member confidently proclaims and leads me off in the opposite direction. We traverse the veld for about a mile before the church building appears from under a majestic mopani tree. Bricks moulded and fired by members of the congregation rise up to window level. The members dug the foundations and laid the bricks before their enthusiasm dwindled. That was the

45

time of violent civil unrest. After a decade the members felt lost and abandoned. No minister ever visited. Communion was not celebrated. However, their enthusiasm has returned and now they are undeterred and their spirits are unbowed by their poverty. Seventy people have gathered on a cold day in the shelter of the half-finished walls. On the other side of a wall, a fire burns. Tea brews, rice cooks, chickens roast. A dozen children rest snugly on their mothers' backs or cuddle in their warm embrace. The older children are eight kilometres distant, away at school. Scripture is read. Babies and adults are baptised. Communion is celebrated. There is singing, praying and dancing. The meal of rice and chicken is served. We break into small groups to share from common bowls. It is a real thanksgiving meal! Mr Tshuma, the church leader, explains the community's hope that these two rooms will serve as a sanctuary for worship and as school rooms for the children of Zompata. Soon they will not have to walk eight kilometres to school, cross two rivers on the way and during the rainy season stay at home because they are unable to ford the rivers. These are faithful people with their faith in God, themselves and their minister. Step by step the people of Zompata are determined to build a place of worship and learning – a house of God.

Tod Gobledale
Zimbabwe

Words

In the beginning, God spoke,
calling all things into being, giving names
to reflect the value of every living creature.
God gave people the gift of words,
to speak freely like God,
in whose image they were made:
the words of old and young,
rich and poor,
kings and leaders,

wise men and poets ...
known and unknown,
in every language –
books and the media expressing
the greatest good and the most powerful evil;
kind, gracious, comforting words,
of warmth and love,
healing, counselling, blessing;
words of integrity;
elusive words,
inadequate to describe
the indescribable;
uncontrolled, abusive words,
words spoken in haste,
cursing, mocking,
belittling, excluding,
destroying;
direct, creative, truthful words,
building up confidence in others;
hollow words, proclaiming 'Peace'
where there is no peace;
empty, meaningless words;
guarded, deceitful language,
disguising truth and feeling;
a mixture of love and bitterness,
generosity and selfishness
from the same mouth;
words, like a tiny flame,
setting light – for good or evil –
a whole forest!
And, when all is quiet,
the still, small voice of God
is heard in the silence.

Maureen Edwards
England

Creating Word, Living Word

Creating Word,
bringing the world into being,
for the starred sky and the songbird that tell of your being,
for peoples diverse in colour and culture,
made in your image, speaking in many tongues –
we praise you.

    Help us to see you at work in the world:
    May our lives tell the Good News.

Living Word,
seen and heard in Jesus, teacher and storyteller,
speaking words of healing and forgiveness,
standing silent in the face of hatred and lies,
crying out on the cross –
we believe in you.

    Help us to hear the cries of the world today:
    May our lives tell the Good News.

Breath of the Spirit,
rushing wind and still small voice,
challenging, changing, making connections,
creating community, encouraging hope,
come among us, inspire us –
we need you.

    Help us to communicate your love:
    May our lives tell the Good News.

Jan Sutch Pickard
England

When Life's Crippled, Flawed or Faulted

When life's crippled, flawed or faulted,
Filled with fear, with folly strewn;
God is here, yet never thwarted,
Loving in dark sorrow's womb;
God is in each widow's anguish,
God is queuing unemployed,
God will in the prison languish,
God will love, not be destroyed.

When life's hopelessness and chaos
Brings the stress that drags us down;
God is here identifying,
Praying with us as we groan.
When our love and life are battered,
When our strength is all but sapped,
When the way ahead is shattered,
Still within God's love we're wrapped.

Love and folly, cross and kindness,
Echo all we know within;
Jesus challenges the blindness;
Penetrates deception's din;
Builds again where all seemed shattered,
Holds us when we fear or fall,
Takes what's left of life, though tattered,
By His love renews it all.

(Tunes: Abbot's Leigh, Bethany or Comforter)

Andrew E. Pratt
England

Adnabod

Ti yw'n hanadl. Ti yw ehedeg
Ein hiraeth i'r wybren ddofn.
Ti yw'r dwfr sy'n rhedeg

Rhag diffeithwch pryder as ofn.
Ti yw'r halen sy'n puro.
Ti yw'r deifwynt i'r rhwysg amdanom
Ti yw'r teithiwr sy'n curo.
Ti yw'r tywysog sy'n aros ynom.

Er gwaethaf bwytawr y blynyddoedd
Ti yw'r gronyn ni red i'w grap,
Er dyrnu'r mynyddoedd,
Er drysu'n helynt a'n hap.
Ti yw'r eiliad o olau
Sydd a'i naws yn cofleidio'r yrfa.
Tyr yr Haul trwy'r cymylau –
Ti yw ei baladr ar y borfa.

Knowing

You are our breath. You are the flight
Of our longing to the depths of heaven.
You are the water which flees from
The wilderness of our anxiety and fear.
You are the salt which purifies
You are the piercing wind to our pomposity
You are the traveller who knocks.
You are the prince who dwells within us.

Despite the consumer of years,
You are the seed which does not speed to its death.
Despite the confusion of our tale and chance,
You are the moment of light,
Whose aura embraces our life.
The Sun breaks through the clouds –
You are its beam on the green pasture.

Waldo Williams
Wales
Translation by Noel Davies

Awareness of God Everywhere

Lord, help me to know your presence, everywhere;
    in the faces of people on the bus on my way to work,
    in the faces of everyone I meet today.

Come between me and all those I work with.
    May I always remember the purpose of my life –
    to do your will.

When I am frustrated, angry, sad, lonely,
    empty and aimless,
give me a sign,
    that in this modern, manic world
    you are still with us.

Give me a sign
    that will show me the way when I am lost,
    when I have too much to do,
    afraid of a heart attack.

Help me to see beyond the immediate,
    to sort things out, to make sense of it all.
Give me eyes to see all that is good in the world.
    Slow me down, that I may feel.
    Slow me down.

William Rutherford
Northern Ireland

Morning Tea

I begin this day, dear Lord,
    as I plug in and switch on my kettle,
    remind me that you are the source
    of all energy, all life, all connectedness.

Let me make contact with my little universe.
As the steam rises from the spout,
    may my prayers rise to you.

As the tea brews,
    may I rest and reflect on you.

As I drink,
    may your spirit refresh me.
        Bless all those who share the pot with me.

William Rutherford
Northern Ireland

Gleanings

When you reap the harvest of your land, you shall not reap to the very edges of your field or gather the gleanings of your harvest.

(Leviticus 19:9)

Our morning walk takes us through the railway yards along the edge of Plumtree, a town in Zimbabwe. Several empty coal wagons line one track. Their cargo was delivered yesterday to the hospital, the bakery and the police station. A few scattered chunks of coal remain. A woman and three small children crouch in the shadow of the wagons. They seem to be searching for something. We near the crouched figures as we cross the tracks. We greet them 'Livukile (you have risen).' 'Sivukile (we have risen),' they reply softly. They each hold a battered basket. The shining, black coal they have gleaned reflects the light of the rising sun.

The poor are always with us. What do we do to help others get what they need? What do we leave behind for others to glean? When we rake the fall leaves, do we leave some behind for the children's enjoyment? What jobs do we create with our wealth? Do we claim the gleanings of our harvests as our personal property and name gleaners as thieves? Do we claim our due and neglect our responsibility to provide what is due to others? The coal in the train yard belongs to the government. Labour is cheap. Every chunk could have been collected. The woman and her children glean from what has been intentionally left behind. They will have fuel for their cooking fire and a bit more warmth for these cold nights.

Tod and Ana Gobledale
Zimbabwe

Carol of the Epiphany

I sought him dressed in finest clothes
Where money talks and status grows
But power and wealth he never chose
It seemed he lived in poverty.

I sought him in the safest place
Remote from crime or cheap disgrace
But safety never knew his face
It seemed he lived in jeopardy.

I sought him where the spotlights glare
Where crowds collect and critics stare
But no one knew his presence there
It seemed he lived in obscurity.

John L. Bell
Scotland

Brought to Life

Jean Vanier: 'I begin to discover something: that this wounded person looks at me, approaches me – all this does something to me, the wounded person calls me forth ... we are brought to life by the eyes and hands of wounded people who seem to call us forth to life.'

On a dusty road,
an outcast, with both hands outstretched,
offered me a blessing.
And, deep within, a child who felt cast out –
unrecognised, oppressed –
found voice, and made a song.

In a shanty town,
one who was in rags, both hands outstretched,
offered me a gift.
And, deep within, a hungry, naked child,
tremulous and needing care,
felt fed and richly clad.

In a hospital,
one who will die tomorrow, hands outstretched,
offered me a healing.
And, deep within, a child who hurt and bled
and felt disordered and diseased,
was held, and helped to dance.

There is a touching place
where those whose wounds are seen
reach out to hidden wounds
behind facades of affluence, well-being,
confidence; and say,
'I recognise you: we are one.'

And some will turn away, afraid
to be unmasked.
And some will weep, at once appalled and glad
to be so recognised; and free
to receive at last and to be heard;
enabled thus to hear and share,

within the commonwealth of woundedness,
the strange, unsettling glory of new life.

Kate Compston
England

Outside the Church

When Abul Khayer, a 9-year-old boy, from Toragarh village under Chandpur went to the railway bridge close to his house to pick up snails for his ducks, he suddenly spotted a broken railway line. He knew that the Intercity train from Hajigaj was coming soon. Then he suddenly remembered that the stationmaster waved a red flag to stop a train. Abul rushed home and returned with his grandmother's red petticoat which he had tied to a stick. He waved the petticoat from the bridge which the driver saw and stopped the train.

More than one thousand passengers got down from the train, heaved a sigh of relief when they saw the broken rail and paid their gratitude to the intelligent and plucky little boy.

'I feel very proud of the deed of my son,' his father said. Sometimes I hear christians sigh, 'Where today is the Holy Spirit working?' We have to realise that the Holy Spirit does not only work in the Church among christians, but also outside the Church. This is such an example of God's generous grace.

Thank you Father!

Bart Baak
Bangladesh/The Netherlands

This Is My Destiny

I am blind. I cannot see.
This is my destiny.
But thank you God,
that through my dark colour,
I can see the wonderful colours of your love.
And I prefer it
To the multiple colours of atrocity
This world is offering.

    I am dumb. I cannot speak.
    This is my destiny.
    But thank you God,
    that through my mumblings I can speak to you.
    And I prefer it
    To the multiple words of nonsense
    This world is saying.

I am deaf. I cannot hear.
This is my destiny.
But thank you God,
that through my deafness I can hear you.
And I prefer it
To the multiple news of horror
this world is announcing.

    I am physically handicapped.
    This is my destiny.
    But thank you God,
    I am still your child
    Whom you cherish.
    And I take it for granted,
    As a special gift
    To proclaim your deep love.

Ranto Ranaivoson
Madagascar

Enable Us To Be ...

Loving, holy One, Kol Yahweh,
    we seek your voice,
    we seek your vigour,
    we seek your stirring,
    we seek your stillness.
Bless this our seeking.
Increase our capacity for You
as the people of the Passionate Realm.

Loving, holy God, Word For Now,
    we hear You call,
    we hear You sing,
    we hear You laugh,
    we hear You cheer.
Bless this our hearing.
Increase our alertness for You
as the people of the Joyful Realm.

Loving, holy Son, Life Offering One,
    we speak your healing,
    we speak your release,
    we speak your vitality,
    we speak your peace.
Bless this our speaking of You
as the people of the Eloquent Realm.

Loving, holy Spirit, Revealer,
we care to find the truth-kernel
    in anger and loss,
    in devastation and danger,
    in discovery and daring,
    in celebration and rejoicing.
Bless this our caring for You
as people of the Resonant Realm.

In this seeking, hearing, speaking, caring
may Jesus Christ enable us to be
spirits who can thrive in the spiritual Realm of God's love.

Glenn Jetta Barclay
Aotearoa New Zealand

Touching

My fingers touch the keyboard all day long.
But that is not the place where they belong.
My hands are happy when in touch with friends,
when saying 'welcome,' 'sorry,'
'be my guests.'
My hands delight in being in the earth,
assisting in a flower or carrot's birth.
My hands are glad immersed in kneading dough.
I share in God's creation that I know.

John Hunt
Aotearoa New Zealand

So Busy

So busy trying to please God ...
         playing church ...
                  serving on committees ...
Walking with cardboard white suits and hats,
Lips painted on faces in the position of a smile,
         Hearts hidden away to break another day.

So busy listening to God that one doesn't hear what God is
         really saying ...
                  or what the people have to say.

So busy playing church that I've forgotten why I came here
         in the first place.

Back in the solitude of my room off comes the
cardboard suit and the painted smile ...

Out comes the Broken Heart.
Split in two, with no one to mend it
except Me and You.

Feiloaigia Taule'ale'ausumai
Aotearoa New Zealand

Jesus Stretched Out His Hand

Jesus stretched out his hand and touched him, and said to him,
'I do choose. Be made clean!'

(Mark 1:41)

Taiwan used to be one of those low-wage producer states for
the developed world, but in the last twenty years it has
become the most modern of places. It outpaces several regions
of Western Europe and North America. One consequence has
been the development of a throw-away culture. Things which
used to be preserved, mended and repaired for continued use
are now tossed out when they show signs of ageing or need of
repair. As people clear out old closets to find room for new
acquisitions they throw away things which have been
mouldering in the dark for decades. That which is outdated is
considered useless.

In my neighbourhood an old woman prowls the piles of trash
which are put out for collection each night. She has an eye for
aluminium cans, plastic bottles, cardboard boxes and old
newspapers. These have an immediate resale value at
recycling depots. When I walk past her house I see collections
of electrical wire and appliances which she collects and sells
more slowly. Once, many years ago, someone left a small
refrigerator on the landing outside my flat. I wanted it out of
the way, so took it to her. She sees the value in things which
others have discarded.

Jesus spent his time among common people and those whom the society of his day had thrown out as useless. The demoniac, the leper and the prostitute all found a welcome from him. By his touch they were healed, cleansed, and valued. In a way, they were recycled. He still recycles people, here in Taiwan and all over the earth.

David Ya
Taiwan

Who Did You See?

Some saw the Baptist,
some saw Elijah,
others a prophet
from long ago
but may we see in each other
the Christ of today.

Richard Becher
England

Seeing

It was easy to see You
in holy faces, holy places,
God made flesh in a mother's voice
or in the gentle hands of a nurse
or the smile of a grandmother
or the laughter of small children.
Every presence of love and beauty
proclaimed Your advent.

I needed eyes sharpened by suffering
before I was able to see You
in the pain of human poverty.
The man who stared at a prison ceiling,
the alcoholic mother, the hungry child,
the old woman who died alone in her flat,

the young victims who grew up
to become abusers themselves,
the people who were in despair
over their inability to make changes,
when I could look at them
through the experience
of my own crucifixions,
I realised that they all looked back at me
with Your eyes.

It took much longer to see You
in places of affluence and power,
in Parliament or at the stock exchange,
or at the helm of a luxury yacht
or residing in a summer palace,
surrounded by material wealth.
But I now discover that in these places
You have the same eyes as the poor,
the disabled, the imprisoned,
the same eyes as my grandmother,
the child, the hospital nurse.

Joy Cowley
Aotearoa New Zealand

God Bless Our Contradictions

God bless our contradictions, those parts of
us which seem out of character. Let us be
boldly and gladly out of character. Let us be
creatures of paradox and variety: creatures
of contrast; of light and shade: creatures of
faith. God be our constant. Let us step out
of character into the unknown, to struggle
and love and do what we will.

Michael Leunig
Australia

The Silent Prisoner

Visiting hour comes around
with regularity
and names are called
and favoured ones
emerge from cells
to see some loved one
through another cell
glass-walled
while others wait
in silence
their names not called
but God sends messengers
beyond the bars
to cheer the silent ones
to throw a rope of hope
to those whose dreams
are lost among the stars.

Harry Wiggett
South Africa

Open Mind

Oh God, may my mind
never become closed by belief
but may it always be open
to the surprise of you,
to the newness of you,
to the woosh of wonder that comes
with the discovery of you
in unexpected places.

Joy Cowley
Aotearoa New Zealand

Celebration

Dear lover of food and wine and fun,
your mirth doesn't feature in the gospels
(Writers never take humour seriously)
but your reputation for the enjoyment of life
sneaks through between the lines
and your cosmic jokes shimmer around us
on even the dullest of days.

Dear lover of parties and people,
we thank you for this gift of celebration
and the way your laughter has touched us
through two thousand years of dinners,
picnics, holidays, festivals, weddings,
dances, birthdays, and reunions,
reminding us that serious concerns
all too often divide us,
that love and laughter heal us
and make us one.

Joy Cowley
Aotearoa New Zealand

The Desert

God, people talk about periods of spiritual dryness. They say that if I can't feel your nearness sometimes, to keep working at it; that the dryness will pass if I don't give up.

Do you want to know something, Lord? I can't ever remember a period of 'wetness'. I mean, as hard as I have tried, I never get the feeling that is supposed to come to me. Am I hopeless? Are you really there listening? Please let me feel your presence just once, so I'll know what it's like.

63

Do you think, God, that I can go on by simply believing with all my heart that you do hear; that it doesn't make any difference in terms of your listening, if I feel it or not?

I'll try it that way, Lord, but you sure aren't making it easy on me.

Author Unknown
Philippines

You Are the God of the Poor

You are the God of the poor,
The human and simple God,
The God who sweats in the street,
The God with the weather-beaten face,
That's why I can talk to you
The way I talk with my people,
Because you are God the worker
And Christ is a worker, too.

You go hand in hand with my people,
You struggle in countryside and town,
You line up in the work camp
To get your daily wage.
You eat snowcones there in the park
With Eusebio, Pancho, and Juan Jose.
And you even complain about the syrup
When they don't give you much honey.

I've seen you in the grocery store,
Eating in a snack-bar,
I've seen you selling lottery tickets
Without being embarrassed about that job.
I've seen you in the gas stations
Checking the tires of a truck,

And even filling holes along the highway
In old leather gloves and overalls.

(Part of the Nicaraguan Mass)

Batahola Choir
Nicaragua

Ordinary Folk

Out of the ordinary comes the extraordinary. We ask, O God,
that you be present in all our doings and our being. Give
meaning and purpose to the common routines of each day.
Give hope and promise to the events that shape us and shape
our world. Give each one an ordinary task and extraordinary
love to carry it out in your name.

Betty Radford Turcott
Canada

From the Depths You Called

In the beginning, Holy One,
my world was without form
and empty
> **no rhyme of routine**
> **no reason to get up**
> **no work**
> **— no me.**

In the beginning
I tried to run from
this yawning void;
But from its depths you called me
to teeter on its giddy rim
to stare into its vortex.

In that swirling chaos, Holy One,
you showed me emptiness
crying to be filled —

the blank and empty page
crying for the writer;
the empty ritual
crying for the liturgist;
the empty pews
crying for the evangelist;
the torn ozone
crying for the earth-healer;
the barren land
crying for the reforester;
the broken heart
crying for the lover;
the chaotic mind
crying for the teacher;
the babble-on of empty words
crying for the prophet-poet.

Now, Holy One, I see in emptiness
the crying need
creating work
  your work
  a new work
  — a new me.

Norm S. D. Esdon
Canada

Be Strong and Courageous

God commissioned Joshua to lead the people of Israel into the promised land after Moses' death. Joshua knew the task would require tremendous courage and leadership abilities. He was afraid. God told him, 'Be strong and courageous; do not be frightened or dismayed for the Lord your God is with you wherever you go.' *

As I stood in the foyer of the Regina Quick Center for the Arts at St Bonaventure University in southwestern New York State, I understood Joshua's feelings of fear and inadequacy. Would I be strong enough to complete the task that God had commissioned me to begin over a year ago?

I let my thoughts drift back over that time. A small group of us had met at a local restaurant to discuss the possibility of bringing a portion of the NAMES Project AIDS Memorial Quilt to our home town. I had been a speaker at a Quilt display in Dubuque, Iowa. After that event I knew that I would be working to bring the Quilt to Olan, New York. God had spoken to me before and now I was to bring His message of acceptance and love to church congregations for people living with AIDS. Would I have the leadership ability to undertake such a task?

As I looked at the colourful banners that decorated the halls and entrance foyer I knew that without doubt AIDS had come home. With God on our side who could fail?

Over four thousand people had come to view the AIDS Quilt panels. Some of the volunteers dressed in white stood at the doors to greet people and hand them red ribbons. Others waited for new panels to arrive so they could be recorded and prepared for hanging. Counsellors were available to talk with guests who requested the service. Everything was going as planned. Well, almost everything. I wasn't prepared for the next scene as I looked up at the panels draped over the railings. I recognised Rosanne and Jerry Meyer with their younger son Justin from New York standing behind one of the panels. They were gently stroking the panel which was dedicated to Randy, their son who had died of AIDS a year before. Justin had made the panel for his brother. My husband Jim and I had visited the Meyer family and met Randy a few months before he died. Randy was a haemophiliac who had been infected with the AIDS virus when receiving transfusions for his illness. He joked with us and we compared stories about living with AIDS; of taking so much medicine and always being tired. Later, when we were told that he had died we went to his funeral and wept with his family. My heart broke again as I watched Rosanne and Jerry hug their son Justin as they clutched the railing holding the panel with Randy's picture etched on it.

*Joshua 1:6

Helen Worth
USA

A Touching Place

Christ's is the world in which we move,
Christ's is the folk we're summoned to love,
Christ's is the voice which calls us to care,
And Christ is the one who meets us here.

Chorus: To the lost Christ shows his face;
To the unloved he gives his embrace;
To those who cry in pain or disgrace;
Christ makes, with his friends, a touching place.

Feel for the people we most avoid –
Strange or bereaved or never employed;
Feel for the women who feel for the men
Who fear that their living is all in vain.

Feel for the parents who've lost their child,
Feel for the women whom men have defiled,
Feel for the baby for whom there's no breast,
And feel for the weary who find no rest.

Feel for the lives by life confused,
Riddled with doubt, in loving abused;

Feel for the lonely heart, conscious of sin,
Which longs to be pure but fears to begin.

Graham Maule
Scotland

Praying in the Market Place

I saw a stranger yestreen:
I put food in the eating place,
Drink in the drinking place,
Music in the listening place;
And in the blessed name of the Triune
He blessed myself and my house,
My cattle and my dear ones.

And the lark said in her song
    Often, often, often,
Goes the Christ in stranger's guise
    Often, often, often,
Goes the Christ in stranger's guise.

In stranger's guise indeed he comes; early in the morning in dressing-gown and curlers, face stained with tears and fingers with nicotine. Today's casualties do not lie only in the ditch on the Jericho road, waiting for us to stop or to pass by, but knock importunately upon our doors, a request for a cup of sugar thinly concealing the need for comfort and someone to share the pain. Christopher Jones, an American poet with an exceptionally acute vision of Christ in his neighbour, writes:

Do not be afraid to see
What is really there.
Do not be afraid of the next day,
the next hour,
the next moment.
There He is.
Do not be afraid of him!

He is a woman old and wrinkled
and smelling like wine, and dirty
with sneakers and a torn sweater and a handbag
cracked and torn,
Smoking a just-rolled cigarette.
Do not be afraid of His language
or the looks of Him
or the smell of Him.
He is your God.

From Listen Pilgrim

Perhaps the ability to see through the disguise, the mask that conceals the suffering Christ, is partly a cultural one. Those who work with the mentally handicapped are in part naturally equipped and in part trained to see the powerless, the scorned, the rejected Christ among those with whom they work. And yet they may be blind to the wretched, lonely, wounded heart so well disguised in the rich woman who cannot bring herself to kiss a dribbling handicapped boy. And yet he is there, he comes disguised in all men, in the long-haired hippy strumming a guitar in the Underground no less than in the dedicated nurse's gentle ministrations. He calls out to us in different voices and in different places, for a smile at the cash desk in the supermarket, or for a patient ear in the train when we would rather read or pray.

And what of all the other workers, and those who have no work? Whatever the pattern of our day, tranquil or chaotic, we can pray if we choose. Those who work with their hands rather than with their heads are perhaps in a privileged position, for their minds are much freer to ponder on the mysteries of God and to pray. Gardening, farming, brick-laying, grave-digging, or crafts such as book-binding, pottery, or printing are often the chosen tasks of men and women who are intellectually equipped for work which is much more demanding. What a terrible 'waste' of talent goes on among the Little Brothers of Charles de Foucauld or in Cistercian monasteries, where men with university degrees spend their working day in factories, tilling the soil or looking after chickens. This is folly indeed in worldly terms, but our system of values is turned upside down by Christ, the folly of mankind becomes the wisdom of God.

Sheila Cassidy
England

The Future Present

A wise rabbi was walking along a road when he saw a man planting a tree. The rabbi asked him, 'How many years will it take for this tree to bear fruit?' The man answered that it would take seventy years. The rabbi asked, 'Are you so fit and strong that you expect to live that long and eat its fruit?' The man answered, 'I found a fruitful world because my forefathers planted for me. So I will do the same for my children.'

The Jewish Midrash

Spirituality

Save me, Lord of sanity,
from a perverse spirituality
which panders to neurosis.
Keep me in touch each day
with the grit of ordinary things:
    magpies sitting on a fence,
    the horrors of war,
    a grandchild on my shoulders,
    the anguish of hunger,
    smiles of strangers in the street,
    tears of the unemployed.
Restructure my hungers
until they intermesh
with the passions of Jesus

and my renewed spirituality
shares in this earthly godliness.

Bruce D. Prewer
Australia

Older and Wiser

From the branches
    of trees once lopped
    the bellbirds chime.
Through valleys where
    I used to rush
    I now find time.
The rambling vines
    I once did curse
    have borne ripe fruits.
Beneath the flowers
    I thought were new
    I find old roots.
In fond theories
    that once seemed wise
    appear deep cracks.
On paths where I
    felt all alone
    I find Christ's tracks.

Bruce D. Prewer
Australia

Lord, We Know

Lord, we know that you'll be coming down the line today, so,
Lord, help us to treat you well, help us to treat you well.

(African-American woman who helped with the weekly
food line a mile and a half from the White House.)
Mary Glover
USA

We Are Going Home to Many Who Cannot Read

> We are going home to many who cannot read,
> so, Lord, make us to be Bibles,
> so that those who cannot read the book
> can read it in us.
>
> (after four months of Bible class in which
> refugee women learned to read)

Chinese Woman

Contemporary Human Beings

Contemporary human beings, whether they have christian heritage or belong to a people that has not known Christ, have a heightened self-consciousness. We need to take this into consideration and not concentrate only on God, for it is also true that as this heightened self-consciousness developed in modern human beings there developed also a sense of their being powerless by themselves. In these criss-crossing, complex and ever narrower paths of the labyrinth of their conscience, they feel increasingly that there is no spiritual way out, and alone they are lost.

Contemporary human beings, in the sorrow of their solitude and the awareness of their own insufficiency, need more than ever someone else to come to them. From their neighbour they want simplicity and purity, that is, sincerity. This should be strong enough to help them to be steadfast in the difficulties and complexities of their lonely life.

Father Dumitru Staniloae
Romania

Even the Stones Laugh

God laughs!

With us, at us and around us!

Give us ears to hear the Divine chuckle,
That reverberates and tickles our ribs and
Grows to a huge belly roar!
A great huge wonderful guffaw!

Give us eyes to witness this holy humour
In our lives
In buckled earth, in cracked character,
In dancing dilemmas and perverse problems.

Give us hearts to mimic our Divine jester
and let laughter oil our lives.

Uniting Church in Australia
National Commission for Mission

God of the Unexpected

God of the unexpected,
You take us by surprise.
For though we're full of knowledge
And feel so worldly-wise,
We sometimes miss your pattern –
We're so set in our ways –
We need your clear directions
To guide us through our maze.

Direct us, Lord, and help us
To see our way ahead,
That other generations
May trace your pattern's thread.

74

Sometimes when you are calling
We cannot hear your voice,
For some work that you give us
We would not do by choice.
Yet when we take your challenge
And cautiously move out,
We find you there before us
To help us through the doubt.

Lord, lead us to the future,
Whatever it may be.
We will trust you completely,
For only you can see.
Lord, you have led so many
Who put their trust in you,
Teach us by their example
To welcome what is new.

God of the unexpected,
You break into our time
To help us take our places
In faith's unending line.
We're part of your great pattern
Of witness, love and praise.
Renew us, Lord, and fit us
To serve these coming days.

Marjorie Dobson
England

Help Us, Lord, To See You in the Dark Places

Help us, Lord, to see you in the dark places,
Help us to see you where you are not easily seen.
We cannot walk forever with the sun on our faces,
We cannot walk forever where the fields are green.

Help us Lord, to find you in the deep shadows,
Help us to find you where you are not easily found.
We cannot walk forever in the sweet scented meadows,
We cannot walk forever on even ground.

It's easy, Lord, to find you in your Bethlehem stable,
Easy, Lord, to find you at your Nativity.
Give us strength and courage, Lord, and so make us able
Still to be beside you in Gethsemane.

Help us, Lord, to find you where the path steepens,
Help us, Lord, to find you where we would not readily seek.
Help us to find you where the gloom deepens,
Let us know your presence where the landscape's bleak.

It's easy, Lord, to find you with our friends all around us,
Easy to find you where we are most happy to be,
Help us to find you where you've already found us,
Help us to find you, Lord, on Calvary.

Brenda Hargreaves
England

To the Poor Man

To the poor man God dare not appear except in the form of
bread and the promise of work. Grinding pauperism cannot
lead to anything else than moral degradation. Every human
being has a right to live and therefore to find the wherewithal
to feed himself.

Mahatma Gandhi
India

For Christ's Sake

Prophets in rags
their property in plastic bags
wine bottles in their hands

walking in our streets
sitting at corners
written messages
open hands

Prophets in rags
searching our dustbins
    for food
not looking at anybody
    not caring
    for anything

Prophets in rags
sleeping in our car parks
cooking on open fires
    sharing
    their food

Prophets in rags
dying in cold winter nights
alone, somewhere
    very near

Prophets in rags
many more of them
not far away.
                    Rudolf Hinz
                    Germany

A Prayer of Longing and Letting Go

You for whom I wait,
unknown, unheard, invisible –
having a thousand names and none –
reach towards me
as I reach out for you;

and be known in the encounter,
heard in the stillness,
seen in the mist and the darkness,
and named fleetingly.
And then
enable me to let go again
of the knowing
the hearing
the glimpsing
and the naming –
content to be poor in spirit
and to travel light,
emptied of all desire
to bind, restrain or define you,
seeking always
to be attentive to you
in the present moment
where you are lively
and new
and always
surprising.

Kate Compston
England

Quaker Meeting

The silence gentles
jagged rocks within,
makes softer the austerities
of pain, gives space
for weighed down shoots
of love to grow up
tall again.

And after the silence,
walking home,
I make connections:

for instance, find
treaties signed between
the countries carved at random
by the puddles on the ground
and territories of my mind's
less arbitrary map: I see
patterns pricked out against the sky
by bare branches
that speak of things
forgotten or laid by:
I glimpse, in the very
carefulness of stones
in a garden wall, a tale
of how we make and break,
are made and crumble –
our strong and fragile selves
conjoined by this
mortality's
strange mortar ...

Fractured by noise,
seduced and continually
by craving to seem useful,
I know my need:
to return over
and often
to this still place,
where roots contorted can
uncurl, where sand
can settle in the hourglass,
where the spirit seems
to glide in cool cloisters,
where listening
and silence are
a potent sharing –
touching us when words
are heavyfooted, bruising

or burnt out –
cradling, steadying, empowering us
beyond the hour of quiet.

Kate Compston
England

Brother, Sister I'm Beside You

Brother, sister I'm beside you,
Let me be as Christ to you,
Pray that I might have the grace
to let you be as Christ to me.

I will listen when you're speaking
I will hear you till you're through
I will grow to understand that
Your ideas are valid too.

I won't rush in to say loudly
That I know a better way
I will think about the meaning
That you're trying to convey.

I will share your problems with you
I'll support you in your space
I will help you run your distance
I will look you in the face.

I will help you face oppression
Prejudice and poverty
I'll identify in your struggles
I will help you to be free.

I'll remember that God made you
I'll not take your dignity

I'll encourage you in your skills
To create and feel and be.

'The Call of Christ'
Aotearoa New Zealand

Be Still and Know

Be still and know
    that I am GOD

In stillness I sought you
    In stillness I felt you
    In stillness I heard you
    In stillness I smelt you
    In stillness I touched you
    In stillness I saw you
In stillness I praised you.

In the insects and the tiger lily I saw you
In the grass and the handshake I touched you
In the roses and the cooking I smelt you
In the laughter and the bird songs I heard you
In the sunshine and the breeze I felt you

I sought you, GOD, I praised you
    All creation enfolded me
        And I knew YOU
          In stillness.

Carys Humphreys
Wales/Taiwan

A Plea

God of the cosmos,
attune our ears to hear you today
in the great symphony of creation.

God of community,
open our eyes to see you today
in the drama of nature's interconnectedness.

God of our hearts,
touch our lives so that we sense you today
in both the beauty and the agony of the world.

Kate Compston
England

A Sower's Farewell

The time has come to move on again,
I feel like a plant that is being uprooted
instead of a sower who cannot stay for the harvest.
The parting would have been so much easier
if we did not come this close.

I was a stranger and you welcomed me
into your barrio and your hearts.
I did not have a home yet I was at home with all of you.
I became a member of your family,
I ate with you and slept in your little huts.
I learned to call you by your names and heard your stories.
You brought me to your farms
and celebrated the ritual of sowing and harvesting.
I went fishing with you
and talked about your hopes
while waiting for the fish.
We went to the swamps
to catch frogs when there was not enough to eat.
You shared with me everything
including your hunger.

The word brought us together.
We listened to it, shared it, lived it and celebrated it,
in your nipa huts,

bamboo chapels, ricefields,
the picketlines and barricades.
The word became alive and was discovered as good news
to the poor and powerless like you,
bad news to the rich and powerful,
and to their uniformed goons.
It broke the culture of silence
and ended the paralysis.
You were able to see the evil around you,
you were able to hear each other's cry,
you were able to speak out and proclaim,
you were able to move, to march, to struggle.
You did not need your coconut wine and sugarcane rum
to give you courage for you were filled
with the spirit.

The military hated us and accused us of being godless
    communists.
They brutally dispersed the picket and the barricade.
Yet it was they who became helpless
for they did not know how to fight
against a people who fought with their tears,
prayers, their songs and their hunger.
We discovered God in our midst
whose will is life not death,
liberation not oppression,
struggle not resignation.
Our lives and struggles became a sacrament
of liberation and salvation.
We discovered our common priesthood
when we drank from the same cup
when we shared the bread of life
and offered our bodies to be broken
for the sake of the kingdom.
Our fiestas have become a celebration of the kingdom
we hope for and struggle for
when abundant food and drink will be shared by all

when only the blood of pigs and chickens will be shed
when only the burst of fireworks will be heard
when we will sing joyfully our hymns of victory
and jump and dance in our land.
Our processions have become our march for freedom
and reminder that we are pilgrims
on the way to the promised land.

Thank you.
I came to evangelise you
but all along it was you who evangelised me
by your life, your faith, your wisdom.
In your faces I see the face of Christ.
You have become a community
of friends and disciples of Jesus
whose liberating mission you continue.

Goodbye.
I came as a stranger
and you called me father.
I leave as a friend and brother.
When the time of harvest comes
remember me.

Amado L. Picardal
Philippines

Jesus Christ Is Waiting

Jesus Christ is waiting,
Waiting in the streets;
No one is his neighbour,
All alone he eats.
Listen, Lord Jesus,
I am lonely too.
Make me, friend or stranger,
Fit to wait on you.

Jesus Christ is raging,
Raging in the streets,
Where injustice spirals
And real hopes retreat.
Listen, Lord Jesus
I am angry too.
In the Kingdom's causes
Let me rage with you.

Jesus Christ is healing,
Healing in the streets;
Curing those who suffer,
Touching those he greets.
Listen, Lord Jesus,
I have pity too.
Let my care be active,
Healing just like you.

Jesus Christ is dancing,
Dancing in the streets,
Where each sign of hatred
He, with love, defeats.
Listen, Lord Jesus,
I should triumph too.
On suspicion's graveyard
Let me dance with you.

Jesus Christ is calling,
Calling in the streets.
'Who will join my journey?
I will guide their feet.'
Listen, Lord Jesus,
Let my fears be few.
Walk one step before me;
I will follow you.

Graham Maule
Scotland

Give Us Hope

Give us hope
to look forward
to happy tomorrows.
Give us courage
to face the hardships
without losing hope.
Give us faith
so that the joy of receiving Christ
will lead us to serve our fellow man.
Give us appreciation
for the gifts we have received
that we might use them responsibly
daring to give
friendship, service and love.
Give us Christmas
throughout the year.

Kim Kwan Suk
Korea

A Time To Keep Silence

Lord,
in a demanding, noisy world
give me moments
when all I can hear
is the sound of a bird
or the rustle of the leaves.
Thank you for time to stop
               time to wait
               time to pray
time to be with someone to whom
I don't need to say anything.

David Jenkins
England

Living Lord

Living Lord,
        you pour out your life for us,
        you pour out your life in us,
        you pour out your life through us.
          Help us to pass it on.

Brian Louis Pearce
England

Listening and Loving

O God, She Came with Flowers

O God,
she came with flowers,
with time to listen.

She came with tears
to shed with me.

She came with friendship
today
tomorrow.

And in her face
your love with me.

John Hunt
Aotearoa New Zealand

We Are Not Meant To Be ...

We are not meant to be
        individualistic
        isolationist
        independent
        insular
but we are meant to live in
        community
        compassion
        commitment
        consensus
        coherence

communication
communion.

Bob Andrews
England

Poor in Spirit

Lord,
    Teach me what it is to be poor
    not just poor with the absence
    of material wealth
But poor in spirit
    the kind of poverty that
    will make me empty
    and create space for you.
Help me let go of the
    false securities, the material props
    that are so easy to cling to.
Show me what it is to be truly bereft.
    Teach me what it is to be poor –
    Then Lord, you will be my all
    and my priorities will be in order –
    Then Lord, I will know what
    it is to truly love.
Teach me Lord, show me what it is
    to be poor – show me, teach me now!

Carys Humphreys
Wales/Taiwan

Suffering Prayer

Lord!
    Teach my eyes to see your love,
    which is not only in the church,
    but also among the people.

Lord!
  Teach my mouth to tell the truth,
  for the people who are being oppressed
  by power structures.

Lord!
  Teach my stomach to suffer
  with people who are hungry
  for food.

Lord!
  Teach my hand to serve,
  for the people who are struggling
  for their lives.

Lord!
  Teach my feet to walk
  with people,
  who need your love.

Burma Issues Staff
Thailand

All It Needs

Just a word,
    just a look
    can heal the hurt
    that people feel.
A silent presence:
    a hug,
    a smile,
    can do the work
    of many words.
The healing power of Christ
    is in our hands,
    in the prayers we say,
    in what we think

and in all we do.
So let your presence be
 the healing that is needed
 in word;
 in touch
 or silent sharing of a grief.
Richard Becher
England

Hush! Take a Moment

Hush! Take a moment.
Listen to the silence.
Breathe in the quiet,
waiting still with reverence.
Deep in the emptiness
we will find our fullness;
hearing the voice of God.

Hush! Take a moment.
Listen to the crying.
People are weary,
lonely, hungry, fighting.
Longing for healing
we will know true feeling;
hearing the voice of God.

Hush! Take a moment.
Listen to the laughter.
Play in the sunshine,
celebrate each other.
Fun bubbling freely,
we will live more joyfully;
hearing the voice of God.

Hush! Take a moment.
Listen to the singing.

Hearts leap with joy
as with your praises ringing.
Love never ceasing!
All to you releasing;
hearing the voice of God.

(Tune: Iste Confessor)

Silvia Purdie
Aotearoa New Zealand

We Are ...

We are a loving people,
   but there can be no love without peace between us.
We are a people of peace,
   but there can be no peace without justice among us.
We are a people of justice,
   but there can be no justice without hope for us all.

Richard Becher
England

God, Where Are You?

Were you listening,
   when your friend spoke;
   did you hear what your neighbour said?
Were you listening,
   to what the stranger said
   and did you hear the words of your enemy?
Were you listening,
   to what people said
   when you met them in the street?
No, I didn't hear what they said,
   I was quietly listening for the word of God.

Were you looking,
   when your friend came to you in pain
   and a neighbour tried to hide her tears?

95

Were you looking,
    when your enemy reached out a hand
    and a stranger cried out for help?
Were you looking,
    at the people all around
    when you passed them on the street?
No, I didn't see them,
    I was busily looking for the light of God.

Didn't you see him, didn't you hear him
    when he spoke through your neighbour?
Didn't you hear him, didn't you see him
    in the presence of your friend?
Didn't you see him, didn't you hear him
    in the suffering of the stranger?
Didn't you hear him, didn't you see him
    in the words of your enemy?
Didn't you see him, didn't you hear him?
    Sorry ... Who?
    God ... you just missed Him!

Richard Becher
England

'Be Still, and Know That I Am God'

(Psalm 46:10)

Be still ...
    and in the quietness, the stillness,
        the silence ...
            listen ...
    listen
        to all that is often passed by,
            unheard, in the rush of the busy life ...

listen ... look ...
    and wonder ...

in awe
at the softest sound,
the smallest detail ...
and in reverence,
give thanks to God, the Creator,
for the marvels of His creation.

Be still, and know that I am God.

For He knows the need
of the human mind and body
to 'Be still'
to have time with Him,
to be nourished,
to be refreshed ...
in the quietness,
the stillness,
the silence
He created ...

Be still, and know that I am God.

Be still ...
and deeply in touch with your inner self,
be aware
of your Living, Loving God ...
whose presence is ever near for you
in your joys,
in your heartaches
in your times of deepest need
to rejoice with you ...
to comfort you ...
to encompass you in His love
and give you peace.

Be still, and know that I am God.

'Alison'
Aotearoa New Zealand

Christian Toleration?

Toleration is often
exalted as a virtue.
I am not so sure.
I know I do not yearn
to be 'tolerated'.

Did the father barely tolerate the prodigal?
Does the father merely tolerate us all?

I tolerate, without much thought,
the motorway at dawn,
stale air in city streets,
siren and motor horn.
I tolerate an icy wind,
I tolerate the daily grind.
I tolerate the miscellany
of pulsating humankind ...

Do I tolerate my brothers and my sisters?

I know I do not long to be tolerated.
I long to be
loved,
understood,
welcomed.

Sue Brown
England

Let My Work Live Again

O Spirit of breathing
space and time,
whose work is an opus
still in the writing,
let my work live again —

when I see only a job-to-be-done,
    let me see my opus-to-be-written;
when I put up with an off-the-rack job,
    let me seek my made-to-measure work;
when my work belittles me,
    let me enlarge it to hold who I am;
when my work shackles me,
    let me find the heart to leave it;
wherever time is punched,
wherever time is money,
    let there be breathing
    space and time —
    time for dry bones
    to recover
    and live again.

Norm S.D. Esdon
Canada

She Did What She Could

(Mark 14:3–9)

She came with a token
– yet nothing was spoken –
her ointment jar broken
to do what she would.
Sweet perfume of caring
on Jesus' head sharing,
for his death preparing,
she did what she could.

    Praise God for her vision,
    despite the derision,
    her mighty decision
    to do what she could.
    May her act inspire us,
    her confidence fire us,

when others require us
to change things for good!

The others at table
were none of them able
to see her as stable,
but both mad and rude.
Quite blind to the woman,
not seeing her human
they laughed at this no-one
who 'did what she could'.

Yet Jesus found power
to face his dark hour
in love she let flower,
so he understood
the worth beyond measure
of this simple treasure
that gives God true pleasure –
she did what she could!

(Tune: The Ash Grove)

John Campbell
England

A Litany of Tears

Lord, teach us to weep
as Jesus wept
So that we can sow peace with tears
and reap with songs of joy.
Send us out weeping, Lord
carrying seeds to sow
And let us return with songs of joy
carrying the fruits of peace.

So teach us to weep, Lord
as Jesus wept.
Richard Becher
England

I Weep

I weep,
but I weep not for myself.

I am but one
of hundreds of thousands
who have suffered so.

One day
our pain will end.

No, I weep not for myself,
but for those
who do not yet know
that the pain they create
does not destroy humanity
and dignity.
Burma Issues Staff
Thailand

You Teach Me To Listen, Jesus

You teach me to listen, Jesus;
I hear the cry of the victims
of Auschwitz and Belsen.
I see the grief in the faces
of those who lost family and friends
in the Holocaust
and I pray that your people, the Jews,
may have security and peace.

You teach me to listen, Jesus;
I hear the cry of the victims
of Sabra and Chatila.
I see the grief in the faces
of mothers who lost their children
in the Intifada.
I pray that your people, the Palestinians,
may have justice and peace.

Holy God, I seek to listen with both ears,
to hear the cry of the Israelites,
to hear the cry of the Palestinians
and to be a friend to both communities
praying that both may know your love and peace.

John Johansen-Berg
England

Ecclesiastes Three

(A version for the epilepsy research team at the
Great Ormond Street Hospital for Children, London, UK)

For everything there is a season, and a time for every matter
under heaven:
    a time to begin and a time to end; a time to develop, and a
    time to regress;
    a time to damage, and a time to mend; a time to take
    apart, and a time to put together;
    a time to weep, and a time to laugh; a time for depression,
    and a time for mania;

a time to throw things about, and a time to pile them up
    again;
a time to be in touch with each other, and a time to be out
    of touch with each other;
a time to look for pieces, and a time to lose pieces; a time
    to keep appointments, and a time to miss appointments;
a time to dismantle hypotheses, and a time to construct
    hypotheses; a time to listen, and a time to discuss;
a time to enjoy work, and a time to be frustrated by work;
    a time for conflict, and a time for partnership.

Janet Lees
England

Creed of a Speech and Language Therapist

I believe in God, Creator, Image maker;
by whom the gift to communicate is given.
From the world's first day to endless eternity,
as the world spins round,
so God continually communicates with us.

I believe in Jesus Christ, Mary's child;
in whom the struggle to communicate is affirmed.
Crucified and Risen, as the Disabled One,
his body the Church, is a disabled body,
for whom the struggle to communicate is a daily reality.

I believe in the Holy Spirit, Sophia, Wisdom,
by whom all our communication is enlivened.
She calls from street corners -
as loudly outside the church as from within
making every day a feast of Pentecost.

I believe in us all,
called to communicate
faith, hope and love
by breath and body,

word and wisdom,
sign and symbol
message and machine.
In the embrace of the Holy One
I seek the fullness of life for all.

Janet Lees
England

Interlocking Circles

A tree falls in Brazil
a child coughs in Sweden
a young man finds work somewhere
a young woman is blown up by a land mine somewhere else.

Interconnecting, interlocking circles,
cause and effect,
the ripples of our actions
flood the universe.

Gulf war syndrome,
leukaemia clusters,
powdered baby milk
    made up with contaminated water,
all instances of the ripple effect
in a global village.

O God, three persons
    in perfect community
help us to own the results of our actions
help us to see the effects of our misuse of matter
help us to heal the wounds of your world
through the power of love crucified.

Kate McIlhagga
England

Lord, as Your Spirit Falls on Us

Lord, as your spirit falls on us
let it be as the first drops of rain
on a parched and barren land:
awakening us like seeds in the desert
to flower and show your glory.
Let it be like the ripples in the lake:
reaching out through minds, bodies and souls.

Each one of us like a stone
thrown into the lake:
our every word and action causes ripples
that affect the lives of others.
Help us to think
before we speak or act,
to listen
to your words to us,
so that our ripples may
stir the calm of complacency,
splash on the face of oppression
and surge through barriers and divisions,
that all the world may come to know
your living water
which satisfies our souls
and refreshes our inner beings.

Moira Rose
England

Just the Way Things Were

Blood trickled down Tam's eroded face,
    A scarlet river winding its weary course.
Past the clouded eyes which registered no pain,
    but showed the hurt of earlier years.
        It was just the way things were.

Turning away, Archie staggered into the gloom,
    clutching his ill-gotten prize with gnarly hands.
Raising the can to his lips – his moment of shame
    was washed away into the sea of oblivion.
        It was just the way things were.

Billy sat motionless – like a statue badly carved.
    His face pitted, back hunched against the wind.
    Gaining warmth from his urine-stained blankets.
    He ignored the violence before his eyes.
        It was just the way things were.

In the midst I stood, rolls and soup in my hands,
    helpless, confused, frightened by all that I saw.
These were the foreigners of my comfortable world.
    I'm unable to cross over – unable to understand
        that this was just the way things were.

John Sanderson
Scotland

Intercession for the Homeless

A meditation which concentrates on the theme of homelessness. It uses two voices,
one of which, Voice One, is a homeless person. It is based on my experiences during a
sponsored sleep-out in the city of Edinburgh, Scotland.

Voice 1 Friday 9 pm – it's been quite a good day so far –
warm and dry. Not much success begging though –
but enough for a few cans and a pack of twenty ...
they help me cope.

Voice 2 God, be with all your children – help us to learn not
to judge and condemn people because of their
lifestyles.

Voice 1 10 pm – I sit on a bench and keep Rab company – he
looks terrible. Last night a gang of youths beat him

up for a laugh. I give him a can and a smoke but we don't talk – we've said it all before.

Voice 2 God, be with all your children – help us to appreciate the small acts of kindness which people are capable of.

Voice 1 11 pm – Rab and I set off for the High Street ... the soup kitchen will be open soon and with luck I may get a blanket for the night.

Voice 2 God, be with all your children – be with those who do your mission throughout our towns and cities.

Voice 1 Midnight – The soup was thick and warm – that'll do me 'til tomorrow. No blanket though. I leave Rab and head for my patch outside the pub – people always seem more sympathetic after they've been drinking. At the weekends I can make quite a lot of money, enough to last the week ... but it's usually gone by Wednesday.

Voice 2 God, be with all your children – help us try to understand the way others live and seek ways to help people experience the fullness of life which your Son, Jesus Christ, offers to all.

Voice 1 Saturday 1 am – I did well tonight. If you hassle people long enough they'll usually give you something – especially young people ... they seem to understand. Time to get some sleep. I head for my usual bush in the park ... looks like rain.

Voice 2 God, be with your children – help us to learn that we need to do more than hand out coins to those in need. Help us to challenge those structures which force young and old alike on to our streets.

Voice 1   5 am – I wake up wet and cold. The cold seems to race through my aching bones making me shiver uncontrollably. I discard the sodden newspaper which has been my blanket for the night and I walk around to get warm. It's now that I feel most alone. I'll feel better when the shops open and I get a drink inside me.

Voice 2   Loving God, be with all your children. Open our eyes so that when we see those in need it is Christ that we see.

John Sanderson
Scotland

It's Not Easy, Lord

It's not easy, Lord,
letting down the barriers
to touch a stranger.
We get embarrassed,
shuffle our feet,
fidget in our chairs
and have to look away.
It's not easy, Lord,
speaking your name.
Friends look at us strangely.
They don't know what to say.
They think we're not normal,
and we want to fit in.
It's not easy sharing
ourselves, our thoughts and feelings,
the people we really are
not who we want others to think we are.

It's not easy, Lord,
getting on with your church.
People embarrass us by the songs they sing,

108

the prayers they say.
They don't listen to what we have to say,
or want us to speak when we need to be silent.
It's not easy being ourselves
loving each other,
being one.

It can't have been easy, Lord,
breaking down the barriers,
touching the leper and the lame,
speaking about the Father
to those who didn't want to listen
or who knew better.
Sharing bread with sinners
made you a fool in the eyes of
those who think they know the truth.
It can't have been easy,
saying goodbye to friends
by sharing a meal
or praying in a garden alone.
So much easier to run away
from the cross and its pain.

But it will become easier, Lord,
as we take the risk and learn the Way,
It will be easier to share
the who and what of us
and what we have been given.

Peter Trow
England

Jesus the Compassionate One

Where is Jesus? Is he not present in the helpless tears of a
mother who watches her child die of poverty-inflicted
malnutrition? Is he not present in the pain of a girl child
prostitute who at thirteen already spends her life responding

to the cruel demands of men? Is not Jesus present in the torn flesh of a girl child who has been raped? Tell me, is he not present in the wounded psyche of a woman who has been battered both physically and mentally in her home ... first as a daughter, then as a wife and then as a mother? Is not Jesus present in the disturbed heart of a woman who has been abused by her priest in the safe womb of the sacristy where she has turned for pastoral care? Where do women find Jesus?

Women have found comfort in the compassionate Jesus. Christ is God's presence in the daily life of women living in a context of struggle. Christ is a friend and confidant. He knows what it is to be a female in a context of exclusion and violence. Jesus is the hope that has sustained women in their suffering. The child-like faith in the Christ who weeps with them is what keeps them living. Christ is the healer and provider of strength and courage.

Women no longer see themselves as victims. They are survivors and they will remain silent no longer. In their struggles for life, and in their resistance to the forces of violence and death, women have found Jesus Christ the liberator – Christ working through, for and with women.

Christ comes to us women today!

This we believe in, that Jesus accompanies us women in our everyday experiences of life and in our struggles to find justice and a violence-free world. It is a faith that knows no boundaries, a faith that sustains us in our struggles for life. Jesus is that theology of life – God with us.

Christ came to us women today,
He celebrated with us our small victories.
A poem we wrote together, rather than spend endless times
    weeping.

A song of liberation we sang together, as we walked another
mile.
A theology of resurrection we wrote together, as we
deconstructed all that is unjust.
A dance of freedom we danced, dancing away all that creates
disharmony and causes us rage.
Christ came to us women today,
He promised to walk that journey with us ...

Christ came to her, my sister, today,
He wept with her as she wept tears of pain.
A poem of love he wrote to her to remind her that God cares.
A song of liberation he sang for her, challenging her to
reclaim her power.
A theology of resurrection he wrote, empowering her to
refuse the theology of sacrifice.
A dance of freedom he danced with her, giving her the
strength to stand up and dance.
Christ came to us women today,
He promised to walk that journey with us ...

Christ came to the church today,
He wept for her seeing her lack of courage and strength.
A poem of love he wrote for her, to remind her of his passion
and compassion.
A song of liberation he sang to awaken her to his message of
salvation for all.
A theology of resurrection he wrote when he called us to live
in right relationships.
A dance of freedom he danced with us, challenging us to
stand up and dance for him.
Christ came to the church today,
He promised to walk that journey with us.

Aruna Gnanadason
India

Modelled on Humour

Our Lord God,
today we thank you for ourselves.
We thank you for the work that has gone into our making.
Thank you for our heads, small or large,
made to keep our brains in.
They are sculpted with amusing faces,
and decorated with ears.
Thank you for our eyes, useful beyond measure,
to help us see how different
are all those people around us.
Praise you for our noses, the centre of our faces,
just right to hold our glasses.
Surely, over noses, you laughed.
Thank you for our fingers, for tender touch and caress,
for working and holding.
Marvellous, versatile fingers!
Thank you for our bodies, in so many shapes and sizes.
They are different, so unique,
revealing both your artistry and your great humour.
From our toes to the tip of our heads,
we are wonderfully made.
And we are all loved by you.
For creating, crafting, loving and redeeming,
We thank you from the bottom of our beating hearts.

May we see, beginning today,
the care and love you lavish
on all those unique people around us.
Then perhaps we may learn to laugh
at the sense of humour you showed
when you made us.

Duncan Tuck
England

Peripheral People

(Luke 4:16–24; 9:57–62)

Peripheral people, tangential embrace,
Fleeting commitment to time and to place.
Touch only lightly, too scared to take hold;
hesitant handshake, afraid to be bold.

Peripheral people
just roaming around:
ephemeral sight
and inaudible sound.

Peripheral people, no landing in sight:
no way of knowing the wrong and the right.
Alien always, homeless in mind,
skirting the pathways that others will find.

Peripheral people
just roaming around:
ephemeral sight
and inaudible sound.

Peripheral people, not forced to conform:
maverick outlook, not old and not worn.
Deliberate disorder, eccentric insight,
word in the margin, incisive new light.

Peripheral people
we need them around:
challenging views
on uncomfortable ground.

Peripheral people can show us the way:
free to believe and courageous to say.
Their glancing connection untainted by form,
uncluttered by rules and encircles the norm.

Peripheral people
we need them around:
challenging views
on uncomfortable ground.

Peripheral people as prophets proclaim:
announcing the good and denouncing the shame.
Freed from constraints of requiring to please:
no need to pander or be on their knees.

Peripheral people
we need them around:
challenging views
on uncomfortable ground.

Stephen Brown
England

Loving Enemies

(Mark 11:9 with 15:12–14; Matthew 5:43–8; Revelation 3:14–16)

Within an alternative set of marriage vows, rich in content is the pledge, 'I will love you when I love you, and I will love you when I hate you'.

At first blush, this seems paradoxical. Until, that is, love and hate are seen to be what they are: both passionate expressions of feelings within relationships. They may seem diametrically opposed in the words that are said, and the intentions that are meant, but they both are based on a passionate involvement.

If there was an expression of selfless-love from Christ, in the torrid time towards the end of Jesus' ministry, no less were there irate expressions of anger from those who sought to destroy him. It was passion on passion: a turbulent time of emotional whirlpools. The love and the hatred together. The absolute opposite of indifference. Both emotions were aroused because the human situation was treated with passionate seriousness. Christ's love was and is the herald for liberty – freedom to be the people God intends. The hatred of Christ's opponents stemmed not least from Christ's message of love and liberty compromising the power and influence of those in authority.

Paradoxical though it seems at first blush, there is complete sense in seeking to vow one to another, 'I will love you when I love you, and I will love you when I hate you'. Those words surely take the vagaries of human relationships fully into account and recognise the emotional reality so that it can be said that it is BECAUSE we care that we can hate as well as love.

But that vow, 'I will love you when I love you, and I will love you when I hate you' is not merely this very clever and concise description of the way things are. It is not merely DES-criptive, it is also PRE-scriptive. It carries within it a pledge that is the healing and wholeness that we seek in relationships: a pledge of love even when hate is welling inside.

Far from being hypocritical, this is precisely the AVOIDANCE of pretence: it is an honest admission of our weakness in our love for one another, while at the same time, a re-commitment to the ideal that is precisely what we should do.

Swords and ploughshares, after all, are made from the same material: the instrument of creation beaten out of the instrument of destruction.

So might the passion of love be moulded out of the passion of hate.

Stephen Brown
England

' ... Not Like Other People'

(Luke 18:9–14)

So who are we?
Do we listen before we speak?
Do we judge before the evidence has been offered?
Do we build bridges or barricades between ourselves and
    others?
Are we those who injure or those who seek to heal?

When we give thanks to God for the good things of life that
    we enjoy
do we remember how easily we take His gifts for granted ...
received as of right ... hoarded instead of shared?
Do we recognise how comfortable it feels to be elusive ...
but how unloving and destructive this can be?

'Living God, flame and fire,
burn from us all that is decayed and dissolute;
Brand us with the marks of your love.

Living God, with the wind of your Spirit
sweep away all that is self-centred and superficial;
Bend us to the shape of your love.

Living God, beneath the shadow of your wings
challenge us to gather the unloved and untended of your
    world:
Break us as the bread of your love.'

Jill Jenkins
England

You Stoop To Fasten

You stoop to fasten the sandals of the Indian peasant;
you delight to reach out your hand to bless the Aborigine
    child;

you challenge with your sharp teaching the rich European;
your gospel draws together old and young, east and west.

John Johansen-Berg
England

The Path of Childhood

Grow, Child, grow,
Crouch not in sorrow shades of darker woe
But joyous stand and blossom in the sun –
Take life's small essence gently in your hand
And, as it leavens with the warmth of love,
Watch wonderingly, that you may understand.

Play, Child, play –
Shy though you be, hide not your face away
But carry life-light in your smiling eyes
That it may shine upon your travelling ...
And so reveal, in detail bright enhanced,
A beacon to your path's unravelling.

Go, Child, go,
Into the world, for there is much to know ...
Life-music sounds if you have ears to hear
Its earth-beat bidding you upon your way –
Pause not in fear – if you have love to give,
Then life is yours for you have learned to live.

Margot Arthurton
England

Love Overcomes All

Be still, be still and know
That in the darkest depths of hidden night
The thickly covered stars still glow –
So nothing think of their obscurity ...

Look now, look now and see
In simple acts the hidden depths of love
Transcending terror, travesty and pain –
Star-penetrating through the dark above.

Be still, look now and feel
Within the shudder of a war-torn breath
Those all-pervading, simple acts of love
Which guarantee pure triumph over death.

Margot Arthurton
England

The Lesson

Tell these things to the child at your knee ...

Tell him in quiet simplicity
In words he can comprehend –

That earth upon its axis turns
In perfect equilibrium,
And the history of the world is held
In balance exquisite
With future's poised infinity.

Tell him that the arteries of man
Which run with blood,
Run also with the molten gold
Of purity and good.

Tell him – the tortuous caverns of the mind
Which ruthless forms of torture can devise –
Make also telescopes to see the stars,
And microscopes to watch the germ of life –
Make scattered notes into a symphony,
A brush of colour into images,
The patient marks of guided pen into the written word

For all to read,
And seamless streams of sound distil to poetry.

Tell him that the eyes in which he sees
The burning flash of hate
Will also overflow with sorrows shared,
Will look on love with endless tenderness,
And reproduce in art
The transcendental beauties of the earth.

Tell him that the tongue which sparks in rage –
Will also speak to him in feverish sleep
And gently soothe his night-time fears away;
Will sing in notes sublime,
And read from stories written on a page
The age-old wisdoms of an ancient Truth.

Tell him – the ears which seemingly ignore
The daily trivia of life's demands,
Will hear the infant's need before he cries,
The rapturous lark ascending to the heights,
The sound of drumbeat echoing the heart,
The sobbing of humanity at war.

Tell him – the hand that fires the warring gun
Will also pick a flower for his beloved,
Return the fallen fledgling to its nest,
And guide from harm his own small wandering son.

Tell him – from the depths of sorrow's pool
Life's joyous fountain will at last arise
In height astonishing –
(And every drop reflect the rainbow's end!)
– That in the blackest darkness of the night
The searching soul will always find a moonbeam
Whereupon to dance;
That in the days of summer storms

The humblest dandelion reflects the absent sun,
And in the balmy garden's velvet dusk
The great pale rose of Peace
Regales the moon's serenity with beauty effortless.

Tell all these things to the child at your knee,
That he may comprehend the equipoise of life,
That he may hear, and speak, and see –
And pass the priceless lesson on
To the child that stands, in time, at his knee.

Margot Arthurton
England

In Affairs of Economics

In affairs of economics
prophet Amos spoke the word;
those who gained from corrupt commerce
closed their ears to what they heard;
money ceased to be a servant,
means of meeting human need,
killed the heart of God's own People
ruled by power of human greed.

In affairs of church attendance
prophet Amos spoke the word;
those who offered tainted tribute
closed their ears to what they heard;
worship ceased to be a service
offered gladly from the heart,
lacked the sacrificial living,
its essential other part.

In affairs of daily leisure
prophet Amos spoke the word;
but the constant background music
closed their ears to what they heard:

leisure ceased to be a tonic
recreating soul and mind,
men and women drunk with pleasure
lost the gift of being kind.

To the soul of every nation
prophet Amos spoke the word;
in our leisure, commerce, worship,
hear the counsel of the Lord:
fear the wrath of holy judgement
self-inflicted by our ways,
let the will of God Almighty
be the ruler of our days.

Bernard Braley
England

Shopping Is Also Work

Shopping is also work as every person running a home as well as earning a living or caring for small children knows only too well. In a wider sense, too, if we take our roles as God's stewards seriously, shoppers collectively are a very powerful group. Where we shop, how we shop and what we buy is a living statement of what we believe.

If we wish to make the statement that we love our neighbour as ourselves, we have to take on board that car-owners' shopping at the out-of-town hypermarket, may close down the corner-shop the immobile find valuable or even essential.

If, when not ourselves on the poverty line, we always go for the cheapest price, without considering that this price is achieved through ethically unacceptable working conditions somewhere in the world, we are making a statement about our understanding of the word 'neighbour'.

If we are reckless or greedy in our claim on natural resources, we may push up the price of a product and make it unaffordable to those with smaller budgets: or ignore entirely the needs of our neighbours or future generations.

Shopping which involves the shopper in making ethical and religious judgements may be nearer to the worship God requires than any number of pious prayers in church.

Bernard Braley
England

Who Needs Words?

If Jesus was the Word
made flesh
for purpose,
why do we smother Him in words again,
instead of reaching out
with loving
suffering hands
to make real contact
with people,
as He did?

Marjorie Dobson
England

When Prophets Are Silent and Faith a Distortion

When prophets are silent and faith a distortion,
The bruised reed lies broken, and hope is snuffed out;
We wander through deserts of fear and deception,
Despised and derided and driven by doubt.

The dry bones of exile lie fallen and broken,
We find ourselves lost in the darkness of night;
The leaders are blinded, by God seem abandoned,
While wrong is exalted as if it were right.

When God loses patience with pastors and people,
Foundations are shaken and hopes are unsure;
The faith which is broken, the love that's forsaken
Are open through pain to God's promise and cure.

He digs up foundations of guilt and injustice,
He opens the pathway to truth from deceit,
From brokenness, nothingness, renders salvation;
This vulnerable path leads to praise that's complete!
(Tune: God's Answer)

Andrew E. Pratt
England

Blossom

Fabric of this love is skin thin
transparency of paper.

Words are written to be certain
of their meaning

even their reading
risks misinterpretation.

Carefully chosen
sounds which shake the roots
of who I am

and even of what I might become.

Valerie Shedden
England

All in a Day's Work

Funeral forms are documents of missed opportunity.
Scribbled names of people who are now shadows of reality.

Spelling carefully, listening to the tale of yet another death.

I find the house, it lies hidden in a maze of streets
whose names are missing or defaced.
I whisper a prayer,
unspecific request
that God will be there.

The bereaved daughter is taken aback,
a woman in black is not unusual, but clerical collars
are a surprise. She swallows her discomfort.

'Come in, sit down, can I make you a cup of tea?'
all in the same breath,
I try to make her feel less at sea
with this welcome to her father's death.

He's in the front room, out of sight,
his face another porcelain figure beneath a dust sheet.

I ask 'How are you?'
Tears surface, her eyes are at the bottom of the sea.

I wait for the dam to break.
She tears the tissue in her hands
shreds his last moments at my feet.

I listen, the only sound the hissing of the gas fire,
it greedily eats the air, suffocates the freshness from her tears.
Dry eyes meet my gaze.
She chooses Abide with Me. Her mother's favourite hymn.
'She liked to sing with the telly on a Sunday night before they
    both went to Bingo,
we sang it at her funeral.'
Another pause as she waves goodbye,
remembers how they always came back.

I let her open the box of her life,
take out precious gems,
hold them to the light.

Epitaphs are made of these.

As she shows me the adornments of her memory,
I start to see flesh blossom on
the bones of love.

'He wasn't great, he wasn't important,
the only thing he knew was birds and leeks,
he laughed at the bairns as they tried to speak,
but never had much to say himself.'

I start to see the wisdom of this man in the other room,
a mansion of huge proportions.

He knew where to hide, he could find peace and quiet,
he found joy in life. He was rich indeed,
that her grief is so deep.

The words come, I spoon them out like honey,
pour them over the flower arrangement which hides the
    wood,
masks the person shape of the coffin.

The people in the back rows stare as if I display their own
    secrets.

If only they knew,
we share the same thoughts,
we all stand here afraid.

I make no mistakes, they weep gently now as I pray,
the words I say are fielded to them for their approval and
    acceptance.

Another silence as we recall the farewell speeches we've ever
    made.

We take the last journey of death,
undertakers in dusty black raincoats
lift him high, shouldering their own pain
as they turn around.

Valerie Shedden
England

Isolated in My Grief

Isolated in my grief,
Broken within by the loss
of my loved one,
Feeling my world
had fallen apart.

A visitor from the local church
called regularly,
She shattered my loneliness
by the warmth of her presence
and smiling face.

The servant of the Lord
listened
and entered my dark world,
Offered me words
of comfort and hope.

Over a period of years
she enabled me to be free
from my isolated prison.
God transformed my world
from darkness into light.

Now I visit people
in similar situations,
Sharing their sorrows
and pointing them
to a new world.

A world where
the springs of tears
can be transformed
into oceans
of loving service.

Believing now
that nothing can separate anyone
from the love of God
in Jesus,
Who offers new life.

Ann Shepherdson
England

I Hear Your Sabbath Rest

I didn't listen, Holy One —
I chose
to keep the sabbath busy
to drag it out of fallow
and lump it with my working six
ravenous
for more business.

O Holy One, you warned me;
Now I reap my foolishness —
instead of more business,
more busyness;
instead of an extra working day,
one more depleting day.
Your seventh day unfallowed

all seven days
all my work
all of me
is exhausted and unhallowed.

Now, Holy One, I listen —
    I hear the musical rest
    out of the din of
    note-after-note-after-note
    creating
    Moonlight Sonata and B Minor Mass;
I hear your sabbath rest
out of the din of my
day-after-day-after-day
making
Kyrie-Gloria-Sanctus of
my week
my work
and me.

Norm S. D. Esdon
Canada

Good Friday

We do not call it Bad Friday
although, for the One who lived and died
the torture of that day
there would have been nothing good about it.
It was death by dishonour,
death by a pain so severe
that it filled all the spaces of thinking,
wrenching forth the cry,
'My God! My God! Why have you forsaken me!'

This One, this Christ who used nature
to describe eternal truths,
who spoke of the cycle of the seasons

128

with images of grains of wheat,
fields, lilies, sparrows, grapes, figs,
fishes, sheep and flowing water,
this One was too steeped in agony
to remember that even the rarest flower
must die to produce a seeding.

But we who bear the gift
of his life and death and life,
call it Good Friday
and carry with us
the knowledge that in Him,
all of our crucifixions
are but resurrections unborn.

Joy Cowley
Aotearoa New Zealand

Where You Are Bringing About Justice

Ay bendito, Jesus. Do you remember the sermon that so much aggravated the lesser gods? I was attempting to describe you as I perceive you in the intimate chamber of my own self.

You are the Lord who, because of your love for us, became poor, even though you were rich. The apostle Paul called that grace. And I feel that he was right because you yourself were the offering, the gift of God that reconciles the world, not taking into account human sins.

These days, when the church is pulled here and there, it is glorious to remember that you did not organise a single political party, that you did not divide the goods of this world, that you did not take that which was not yours, that you did not take away from each person's worth. On the contrary, you were poor, you identified yourself with sinners like myself, you offered yourself as a mediator, you gave yourself without reserve, and you sacrificed yourself on a cross in order to

129

redeem us from sin, 'that those who live might live no longer for themselves but for him who for their sake died and was raised.'*

If we intend to identify ourselves with you, we cannot live removed from the processes of this world. We cannot turn a deaf ear to the clamour of a world that expects a sign from God's children. We must take the flag of justice and make it our own, so that we can be instruments of peace.

And so we must be alert to the processes of change to be sure that we will go where you are, bringing justice about so that we will not be confused with sterile fantasies.

We're working on it, and we'll see each other around, Lord, on the road.
*2 Cor. 5:15

Juan Marcos Rivera
Puerto Rico

Reflections

A group of people need to sit in a circle.

Place in the middle of the circle: a packet of painkillers, a small piece of aluminium, an empty aluminium can (made from bauxite), coffee, sugar, bananas, a picture of a building being constructed and a tourist brochure of The Caribbean.

(Refer to 1 Kings 21:1–6 and Mark 6:30–42.)

As you look at the items in the centre of the circle can you share what use they have in your society? Are you aware of where the items come from? Are you aware of the working conditions in the pharmaceutical industry and other factories where these items are made? Are you aware of the agreements between your country and countries in The Caribbean?

Whom do they benefit?

As you read the narrative of 1 Kings 21:1–6 you learn how powerful greed can be; it can take the life of a human being. Greed now takes the lives of many people. Greed has been disguised by claims that pretend to account for our well-being as a nation. The narrative in Mark gives another perspective on humanity. People come to see Jesus and they are like sheep without a shepherd. Even with the reluctance of the disciples to care for them the words of Jesus are clear as he insists that they have something to eat. The act of giving in the gospel is not like the giving of international aid that takes more than it gives. It is a giving that becomes a sharing of all that we have.

When we share we receive what we need and there is some left over for those who have not yet come. What can you as a church share with the people of The Caribbean? What can your nation share with The Caribbean? Do you agree with the international policies that determine the way that your country gives? Are you prepared to propose a different way of giving and a better way of sharing?

Leader Help us, Lord, to understand your ways and not ours; to see in sharing the bread of the world your will; to overcome the temptation of greed and avarice and become people who give to others.

People Help us, Lord, and give us strength.

Leader Forgive us for the ways we have taken that reveal our indifference for others and our lack of trust between one another.

People Forgive us, Lord, and grant us your power and renewal.

Leader The Caribbean people have suffered discrimination, racism, economic deprivation, cultural isolation and social inequalities. Help us to take their struggles against these sins as our own struggles. Allow us to experience your power in solidarity.

People Grant us the opportunity to serve in your name. Grant us the opportunity to see you, Lord, in our brothers and sisters from The Caribbean. Grant us the opportunity to live together as a community of faith, hope and love.

Carlos F. Cardoza- Orlandi
Puerto Rico

For You, Tourist

For you, tourist.
Roaming to and from among our islands
You've enjoyed our surroundings
Discerning nothing of manifold impacts
entering into the land we love.

You've pleasure in sightseeing our cascades,
fresh pools, black and white beaches.
Knowing nothing, your nakedness
and your swimming clothes
are totally evil in our context.

On the street opposite sex hug each other,
holding hands or absurd kissing.
For you, tourist.
Open romances not normal in our culture.
It's a worse crime in our mentality.

You've worn your underwear in town,
You've walked while lapping an ice-cream.
For you, tourist.
These are out of bounds
in our community.

You've left our land
leaving us and our children,
a bitter new model.

132

For you, tourist.
Adjust yourself to our ways
before you tour the land we love.

Fepai F. S. Kolia
Western Samoa

Darning Spirit

She sits working,
needle and thread in hand.
The coat of many colours,
torn and tattered,
is held tenderly across her knee.
She works carefully.
With each hole she anchors her thread,
then weaves together the fragments of cloth,
recreating the pattern.

It must be strong, yet supple,
so well integrated into the fabric
to be almost invisible.
A humble art.

And all the while she sings,
her blessing of peace and beauty
holding all together.

Your church is torn and tattered, Lord.
Come, mend us,
darn us together again
into one, wonderful
whole garment of praise
for all the world to wear.

Silvia Purdie
Aotearoa New Zealand

We Need Your Mother Love O God

We need your mother love O God to keep and hold us tight,
We need your mother love O God to lead us through the
    night.
We need your Holy Spirit to comfort and to guide,
May she give us courage to do what is right.

We need your mother love O God to teach us how to live,
A love that never forces but draws because it gives.
May we reject the pride that thinks we are the best
And that we deserve much more while others can have less.

We need your mother love O God to teach us to say no
To all the ways of violence, to all the ways of war.
Forgive us for the way we have supported evil deeds
Done in the name of our nation while we've simply kept our
    peace.

We need your mother love O God to teach us to say yes
To all the ways of beauty, to all the ways that bless
To be gentle with creation and all God's creatures too
To treat the earth with kindness, to cherish and renew.

We need your mother love O God so we're numbered with
    the meek
Forgive our need to dominate over poor and weak
And men over women and race over race
Forgive us for the fear that hides the human face.

We need your mother love O God to keep our spirits true
To the values of your Kingdom, to the attitudes from you.
Blessed are the merciful, blessed are the meek,
Blessed are the humble, blessed are the weak.

Garth Hewitt
England

134

A Friend Is One Who Comes To You

My mind is racing as I sit here writing my thoughts. There are times I feel my head will explode. Joy, anger, stress, happiness, hatred, peace.

Some while ago I read an advertisement about a unique gift shop. I wrote to enquire about the products that were available and received a response with an invitation from the owner to visit the shop. I discovered it was a lovely gift shop in a small resort town on the shores of one of the Great Lakes, Canada. It was filled with Eskimo carvings, Indian art, English china and the most elegant Scottish crystal. The owner was a very pleasant, kind and interesting individual.

As the months passed I visited the shop a number of times and began to develop a friendship. As the friendship grew into a relationship we discovered we had many interests that were so alike it was frightening, at times. Two years into the friendship he was diagnosed HIV positive. He sat me down to tell me concluding with 'If you want to walk away I will understand.' My response was that 'I could never live with myself if I walked away.'

The three and a half years that followed were filled with highs, lows and in-betweens. There were many great indignities that he had to suffer. Being labelled was hard for everyone but so embarrassing and stressful for him. In the early years of the disease everyone was so frightened and panicky. They forgot about the feelings of the patient. Many hours were spent waiting in doctor's offices; waiting to be the last patient in the dentist's office because of contamination fears; waiting for blood tests and t-cell counts; trips to the drug stores for seemingly endless bottles of pills; waking every four hours to take AZT; long stays in hospital during relapses; endless medication of intravenous drugs; changing the bed and night clothes because of excessive sweating. The list goes on and on and on ....

In the midst of all these depressing and stressful times there was much joy and happiness. Seeing him recover, listening to his words of courage, watching him grow strong, hoping for the slight chance he might be the first to beat this hateful disease. Summers at the cottage, trade shows, Christmas shopping trips, rose gardens, cocker spaniels, stamp collecting, birthdays, touching, hugging, listening, praying, hoping.

However, I was filled with sadness and anger when I saw what was happening to him because of his 'friends'. Their absence was very obvious. When approached the excuse for not visiting or calling was 'Well, I want to remember him as he was' – such a weak and lame excuse. For those of you who read this story, please don't ever be guilty of using that line as it is most hurtful.

Hospice was wonderful. The persons working there were the kindest, gentlest, most caring people on this earth. We knew we were in the last days of his life but there was a joy and peace never previously experienced during the time of medical treatment. We both knew that the calm and safety of hospice would protect us through the sadness we were ultimately going to face. Saying goodbye is never easy but having the calm atmosphere of the hospice and the understanding staff made the process less burdensome.

We are living in a time that saddens me because there are so many shallow, self-centred, self-serving, callous would-be christians preaching the greatness of God and yet treating their fellow humans in a manner that would embarrass Christ. Being so pompous as to believe that they have a right to judge others based on their christian belief boggles the mind and pains my soul.

I am thankful to God for giving me the challenge; for giving me the inner strength to endure; for filling me with the courage to go on. I am thankful for the opportunity to know and love a very special person who will live in my mind and world for the rest of my life. Thank you, Sidney, for being my friend and companion; I love you and will never forget you.

John
USA

Enthusiasm for Life

This story about my only son, Robert, is written with strong conviction and determination for the legacy this young, brave man left behind. I often think of the past with its busyness of bringing up a family. I remember trivial things that were most important at the time but now seem so unimportant. Along with the emptiness, I recall the wonderful memories.

Robert, an ordinary boy, grew into a young man with a zest and purpose for everything he could possibly imagine that life had to offer. Unfortunately, he was struck down in the prime of his life at thirty-five years. He was denied the chance to find and explore, totally, his dreams, yet, at such a young age he had already touched many people with his enthusiasm for life and sometimes with the knowledge of a person twice his age.

Robert grew up in a traditional family with his parents and three sisters. He graduated and left the area, aged nineteen, as an admitted gay man. He was certain to find acceptance for who he was more easily in other parts of the country as his home area stood still in accepting alternative ways of life.

He was diagnosed HIV positive shortly after his 30th birthday. I will never quite realise how I got through the rest of the day after he had broken the news to me. I wanted to scream but nothing would come out, no crying or anything that would get me out of that time. We cried together as mother and son. He was going to die. We had thousands of telephone conversations over the next five years and Robert returned home for family visits and special occasions. His last time home included Christmas preparations and festivities.

Eight months later I was on my way to Portland, Oregon. He had been suffering with severe headaches and periods of blurred vision. He did not want to worry his family needlessly but his loving partner, Frank, called us for help. The next two months of Robert's life were spent with quiet visits to friends and places he loved in the northwest. He often said that it is God's country and he was never going to leave. It gave him tranquility and peace. He discovered Eastern methods of medicine such as herbs, acupuncture and shiatzu which I am sure helped prolong his life. Robert became a walking medical dictionary when it came to the AIDS virus and he left a medical library of information which has been donated to the Grand Island Religious AIDS Information Network. On Monday 30 October 1995 Robert came to the end of his long and brave fight with AIDS. He left this world with the hope that there will be more understanding, compassion and finally a cure for this killer.

Joanne Urtel
USA

Living with AIDS

(An extract from the Memorial Service leaflet for Robert Urtel)

My name is Robert Eric Urtel. I was born in Kenmore, New York on August 26, 1960. I was named after my father and everyone said I was just like my mother. After graduation I became a world-class waiter and culinary expert in some of the finest restaurants in the USA. I had my own house cleaning business while living in San Francisco. My major hobby is catering and I enjoy cooking gourmet dishes. The last two years I've enjoyed living in Portland, Oregon and sharing my retirement with my long time loving companion, Frank Garoutte; better known to me as Francis and me to him as Bobbie. On October 30, 1995 my fight with AIDS came to a conclusion. My hopes are for my family and friends to be enthusiastic for life. My wish is for you to have a smile in your heart when you think of me. Bye for now until I see you next time.

Contributed by Frank Garoutte
USA

Compassionate Spirit

Compassionate Spirit,
    awaken in us a loving spirit
        sensitive to the needs and cries
           of the needy in my village
              and in the whole world.

Divine companion,
    walk with us as we resist
        the powers of evil.
           Direct our paths to
              the way of peace and justice.

Loving God,
    we commit our thoughts and emotions,
        we commit our dreams and visions,
           we commit our work and play,
              we commit our purse and prayers ...

To You, in the service of our people,
    right here in our community;
        in the name of love,
           in the name of solidarity,
              and cosmic interconnectedness.

Oh God of justice,
    bless our awakening and communing;
        as we struggle and resist
            may the beads of hope remain strong
                in our hearts now and forever more.

Elizabeth Tapia
Philippines

Refugees

Compassion

Suffering, sharing
The pain.
Knowing within oneself
Some of the cost.
Spurred to activity,
One hand stretched out
To those who suffer,
One stretched out to
God, who suffers too.
Nothing sentimental:
The sharp edge of love,
Like crucifixion.

Refugees

They stream across our screens
Balancing impossible burdens;
The remnants of their lives
Tied up in bundles.
Yet what we see is nothing
To the burden they carry
In their hearts:
Loss, pain and fear.

Asylum Seekers

They live under the shadow of
A two-edged sword: in a place of safety
And a state of fear. The rules
Ensure we are kept safe; our fear
Defines our hospitality, keeps them on edge.
Compassion is constrained by
Prudent care.

Could we, instead of seeing problems,
Begin to recognise the gifts they bring,
And be enriched by their humanity?

Why them?

God, you must weep to see
The massacre of different
Innocents.
Stick limbs on swollen bellies,
Faces old before their time,
Skin stretched on grinning skulls.

We sit before the screen
And watch them die;
And from the world,
Mingling with your tears
Comes Rachel's anguished cry
Because they are not.

And we could have helped.

Ann Lewin
England

Doctor with the Poor

Dr Edric Baker, from Aotearoa New Zealand, often lives on his
own without support from an organised mission organisation.

Who cares – when one lives with the poor as their brother – the need will be small. He arrived in Bangladesh as a volunteer 10 years ago. His medical treatment programme is varied – community health, tuberculosis, diabetes, cholera and many other ailments under the sun – in the remote tribal village of a big reserve. There is no electricity or running water. Cooking is by wood fire. The set up is simple; the wards are mud houses and patients sleep on mats on the floor. The rural poor, including boys and girls, with little education are the workers. They have gained confidence and efficiency and the place is flooded with patients from far and near. Garo tribal people do not like modern medicines. They often have their exorcists, with doctors, even though many of them are christian. Recently, I was asked to scold a church leader, who brought his two sisters to Dr Baker, at last, when they were dying after treatment with all kinds of local medication. This is often the case. He is the doctor with the poor and they have great faith in him. They tell me that he might be a bit cracked in the head. And I assure them that it is so and for this reason he is with them there. He loves them and loves his Lord dearly.

Bishop B. D. Mondal
Bangladesh

Religion

The preacher was more than ordinarily eloquent and everyone, but everyone, was moved to tears. Well, not everyone exactly, because in the front pew, sat a gentleman looking straight in front of him, quite unaffected by the sermon. At the end of the service, someone said to him, 'You heard the sermon, didn't you?'

'Of course I did,' said the stone-like gentleman. 'I am not deaf.'

'What did you think of it?'

'I thought it so moving I could have cried.'

'And why, may I ask, did you not cry?'

'Because,' said the gentleman, 'I do not belong to this parish.'

Bishop B. D. Mondal
Bangladesh

Gentleness

After a telephone conversation with a very gentle friend, I got to thinking how very valuable is the quality of gentleness. Through the ages poets have praised it in men and women. It would be a tragedy if this loveable quality was lost in the rough and tumble of everyday living. We must consider the stressful needs of today; the need to stand up for one's right, to make noise in order to be heard, to compete in an aggressive, competing world, but we should try very hard to keep the gentle touch. Sorting my Granny's belongings made me remember her gentleness. Her firm but gentle touch for sore knees and the forgiving hug for minor sins. The lovely lavender, rose pink, soft blues and silvery-coloured clothes and the pink and white cameo brooch were so like her – strong but gentle. My mother too, through a short, tough life, was where our friends and neighbours brought their troubles. She didn't blame or criticise – she gently gave them comfort and support. We should never confuse gentleness with weakness. It doesn't mean always giving in and being doormats. We need God's gentle strength to deal with the harshness we meet, without becoming hard. This inner strength means understanding one another, meeting despair with hope, and disappointment without becoming bitter or disillusioned. We should use our setbacks and unhappiness to make us kinder and more understanding. On the occasions when we must stand firm, be brave. By loving others more than themselves, the gentle ones steal our hearts and we love them. Try not to lose the gentle touch.

Derryn Best
Aotearoa New Zealand

Eat and Drink

'Eat and Drink, remember me.'
Peace and love embraces me.
Pressures, tensions, melt away,
Home and still, the end of day.
Flowers have flowered all day long.
Birds begin their evensong.
Books and tapes are at my side.
God's warm arms are open wide.

John Hunt
Aotearoa New Zealand

Jesus, Source of Life

Jesus, Source of life
The only reason for grace,
Fill our stony hearts
With your tender love.
Drop in the true life of yours
To make us love one another
Just the same way as you love us.

Change our unkindness into fraternity,
Our hatred into love,
Our fear into courage,
Our weakness into strength,
Our curse into blessing.
Real instruments of Your Love
Shall we be for ever.

Malagasy Hymn
Arranged and Translated by Ranto Ranaivoson

Called to Account

There's something that I'm feeling
that I can't quite understand.

144

It's to do with the things we say
    and the words we use.
Do they compliment our hearts,
    God's plan?

We talk about listening to the stories of others
    and solidarity with the oppressed
but we continue to speak exclusively
    and fail to recognise
        when we oppress.

We can become so caught up with tomorrow
    that we forget about today;
the mothers of the unborn children,
    the bearers of our joys and pain.

What can we do to give voice to the voiceless,
    to empower the dispossessed?
How genuine is our compassion,
    our ability to confess?

Are we moving in the right direction,
    or have we wandered off the track?
Let's keep discerning the voice of God,
and allow the Holy Spirit to bring us back!

Feiloaigia Taule'ale'ausumai
Aotearoa New Zealand

Loved by God

God of love, we come into your presence aware that you love us from everlasting to everlasting. Your love touches us in all of our being. Before we were born you loved us and your love will follow us to the end of eternity. Fill our lives with your spirit and help us to love as we are loved.

Betty Radford Turcott
Canada

God of Hope

God of hope, touch our lives and our living with your spirit of love. Make our lives places where the flower of compassionate love blooms each day. Help us to love our neighbour, regardless of who that neighbour may be or where we meet. Fill our lives with the love that never lets us go.

Betty Radford Turcott
Canada

Challenge the Normal

In a famous Indian movie an attempt was made to present an unconventional theme. The central character is a lorry driver. He kills a young villager by reckless driving whilst under the influence of alcohol. Eventually, the court of justice passes a stunning verdict!

The lorry driver has to carry out his sentence in the same village, under the same roof, with the young villager's family. Initially, the convict is not accepted by the family because they see him as a murderer. As the story continues the convict gradually learns about the problems and difficulties he has caused by killing the only bread-winner in the family. He undergoes a painful self-realisation and begins to take upon himself the many responsibilities of the family. Also, the anguished family members begin to change their attitude of hatred by expressing forgiveness and love.

The climax is very emotional. The convict, having completed his sentence is set free by law but he refuses to leave the family because he realises that he has to shoulder so many responsibilities and unfinished tasks as a member of the family. He came to the family as an enemy but earned a place in their hearts as a friend.

The movie attempted to negotiate with the humanity of a convict and challenged the conventional norm of any judicial system. I wonder how Jesus would have reacted in His response!

Harold Williams
India

Contact

Reach out my hand to touch
My neighbour, friend,
Or kith and kin.

Not quite;
Not far enough;
The gap's too great.
So I must lean,
Further and further,
Hand stretching out to hand.

What if I fall;
Lose balance and
                    Upset
My equilibrium?

Perhaps I shall have to change my ground.

But do I stand on holy ground?

Donald Hilton
England

God Is Not Only Fatherly

God is not only fatherly,
God is also mother
who lifts her loved child
from the ground to her knee.

The Trinity is like a mother's cloak
wherein the child finds a home
and lays its head on the maternal breast.

Mechtild of Magdeburg
Germany

Self-giving Love

(Ruth 1:16)

Lord, you have told us
that we must be ready to lose ourselves
if we are to find ourselves;
should we ever
be faced with such a choice
as confronted Ruth,
give us grace
that we may also choose
the way indicated by
a loving and compassionate heart.

Edmund Banyard
England

Facing the Truth

(to be adapted according to historical situation)

God,
help us to face the truth about ourselves
and our history.

*It is hard to come to terms with the fact that your church has been
part of the story of Aboriginal dispossession in this land (Australia).
We have been party to policies of government that saw the taking of
children away from their parents as acceptable.*

God who was born into our world
You show us that location is important.

Where we sit determines what we see
Who we sit with affects what we hear.

Help us to sit
with our Aboriginal sisters and brothers
hear their pain
and weep with them
for what was done in your name
that has caused anguish, pain and sorrow.

Free us from the attitude that still lingers that we know what
is best for Aboriginal people.

In facing the truth about ourselves and our history
set us free to new relationships
that are built on trust and understanding,
respect and dignity.

Uniting Church in Australia
National Commission for Mission

Christian Love

Christian love is the 'possible impossibility' to see Christ in
another person, whoever he or she is, and whom God, in his
eternal mysterious plan, has decided to introduce again into
my life, be it only for a few moments, not as an occasion for a
'good deed' or an exercise in philanthropy, but as the
beginning of an eternal companionship in God's power, which
transcends the accidental and the external in origin and
intellectual capacity, and reaches the *soul*, the unique and
uniquely personal 'root' of a human being, truly the part of
God in him. If God loves every human being, it is because he
alone knows the priceless and absolutely unique treasure, the
'soul' or 'person' he gave every human being. Christian love
then is the participation in that divine knowledge and the gift
of that divine love. There is no 'impersonal' love because love
is the wonderful discovery of the 'person' in the 'human

being', of the personal and unique in the common and general. It is the discovery in each human being of that which is 'loveable' in him or her, of that which is from God.

Father Alexander Schmemann
USA

Humanity ... Inhumanity

What is man,
Who, in his inspiration,
Can paint the spark of God upon a chapel roof,
And leave a song of symphonies
Upon the earth?
Who, faced with Nature's mightiest creation –
Will scale the heights with courage to the end,
And still extend, in quiet humiliation,
A helping hand unto his weaker friend?

What is man,
Who in retaliation,
Relinquishes nobility, and to the depths descends
Of infinite depravity
Without a thought?
Who, for the sake of colour, creed or nation –
Fanatical unto his dying breath –
Leads prisoners out, and for extermination
Sets dogs on them to tear them all to death?

We may share with man his mighty aspiration ...

But we must also bear his shame.

Margot Arthurton
England

Where the Song Seeks the Singer

Before the beginning, Holy One,
when you were searching for a job
all was void and darkness.
So you created time and space
where you were needed —
a world seeking you
as you sought it:

> **galaxy seeking star**
> **as star sought galaxy;**
> earth seeking the sun
> as the sun sought the earth;
> **electron seeking proton**
> **as proton sought electron.**

You created a world

> of the seeker and the sought
> **of lover and beloved**
> part and counterpart —
> **each seeking the other.**

In searching for a job, Holy One,
let me seek only the work
that's seeking me.
Remind me who and where I am —
made in your image and living
in your time and space,
where the sought also seeks the seeker:

> the landscape, the artist;
> **the spawning ground, the salmon;**
> the earth, the acorn;
> **the rose, the bee;**

where the song seeks the singer

> **as the singer seeks the song.**

O Holy One, let me sing only
the song that sings me.
Let my work sing out

as yours does —
'I am who I am'.

Norm S.D. Esdon
Canada

Perceptive Soul

Penetrating, warm eyes
   quietly observe
     and absorb
  all that is seen
    and more beyond.

Searching, thoughtful mind –
  a threat to
    the hard wall of defence –
  seeks to cultivate
    trust and credibility.

Firm, gentle hands,
  patient and understanding,
    ever ready
  to sift through
    the crumbling fear.

Perceptive soul bides its time.

Carys Humphreys
Wales/Taiwan

Bridge of Peace

Reconciler God,

We need your forgiveness for our failures in imagination:
we lack the planner's vision to see
  where a bridge of peace could be built.

We need your forgiveness for our failures in perception:
we lack the architect's sense of how
   a bridge of peace might be proportioned.

We need your forgiveness for our failures in stamina:
we lack the builder's patience for constructing
   a bridge of peace stone by stone.

   In confessing our failures
   we find ourselves released
   we find ourselves equipped
   we find ourselves ready –
      ready to be peace-makers:
      planners, architects and builders of bridges.

Kate Compston
England

I Want To Live

I want to live
... and not to die.
I want to laugh
... and not to cry.
I want to feel the summer sun,
I want to sing when life is fun.
   I want to fly into the blue,
I want to swim like fishes do,
I want to reach out friendly hands
To all the young in other lands,
   I want to laugh
   ... and not to cry,
   I want to live
   ... and not to die.

A Child from
Chernobyl

Aboriginal Justice

Bapa (Father), Ngandi (Mother)
You gave us the dreaming
You have always spoken to us through our belief.
You then made your love clear to us
in the message of Jesus.

We thank you for your care.
You own us, You are our hope!
Make us strong as we face the problem of change.
Help the people of Australia to listen
to us and respect our belief.
We can only know ourselves in our culture.

Make the knowledge of you grow strong in all people,
so that you can find a home in us,
and we can make a home for everyone in our land.

Anne Pattel-Gray
Indigenous Australia

Forgive Us for Our Worship

Lord of every facet of our lives,
forgive us for our worship.
When you desire all of us,
we bring you just a part.
We come with a facade of expression and appearance,
but not our real selves.
We pigeon-hole worship, and so fail you.

You call us together for sharing,
to explore our failing and weakness,
and offer it all to you.
You call us together for acceptance,
understanding and love,
to welcome those who are afraid of themselves.

Forgive us.
We do not offer acceptance.
We demand where you do not.
We lay down conditions when you just open your arms.
We accept only a part,
and so withhold wholeness from our neighbour in need.

Thank you,
that you accept us as we are;
that you love us as we are.
So may we love those around us.
By your Spirit may we hold hands.
May we rejoice with the rejoicing,
weep with the weeping.
And may we offer our all to you, together.
Then we may be ourselves.
Then we may be one.

Duncan Tuck
England

Compassion Is the Fulcrum

Compassion is the fulcrum
For the lever of God's love;
Compassion offers insight
When human minds reprove.

Compassion spurred the Godhead
To a life in Galilee,
Incarnate in our suffering
To set all people free.

Compassion moved a stranger
When blind hatred could not see;
Compassion still can move us
To love humanity.

155

Compassion held Christ captive,
For Jerusalem he cried;
For liberty he fought there,
Outside her walls he died.

Compassion is God's answer,
Sets the broken, fallen free
Spurring love to understand
And open minds to see.
(Tune: God's Answer)

Andrew E. Pratt
England

Love Soars Where Eagles Cease To Fly

Love soars where eagles cease to fly,
Love sounds the grief beneath a sigh,
Love ponders how or why,
Love always lives.

Love sings when silence chills the air
Love stills when chaos shatters care,
Love understands our calm despair,
Love always lives.

Love enters into joy and pain,
Love fills the dead with life again,
Love will endure, will still remain,
Love always lives.

Love joins our hearts and minds as one,
Love shares our grief, our joy, our fun,
Love works, love's work is never done,
Love always lives.

Love offers insight to our care,
Love breathes compassion through the air,

Love thrives when life is foul or fair,
Love always lives.

Love values colour, light and shade,
Love loves the gifts that love has made,
Love brightens life, will never fade,
Love always lives.

(Tune: Almsgiving)

Andrew E. Pratt
England

Quietness

The still small voice speaks yet,
We do not hear.
Too busy with our rushing,
Wanting, asking.
Listen to us Lord.

But into the silence
Trickles the voice of God.
Open our minds and hearts,
Speak to us as quiet water
Cool mountain stream
Refreshing, renewing.

Impatience banished,
Waiting in silence
Help us prepare
Our minds and souls
Ready for Advent
Coming of Christ.

Lesley K. Steel
Scotland

Circle Me

O God,
circle me with your loving spirit,
keep fear without and calm within,
keep fear without and hope within,
keep fear without and love within.

John Hunt
Aotearoa New Zealand

Serving and Setting Free

Shake Off Your Slumber

The night so chill and sombre
At last is driven away.
So now, shake off your slumber
For you are the Lord of the day.
Unwind the dreams that bind you,
Now morning's in the air!
Leave barren walls behind you;
March proud in the public square.

Let winds of change be active,
No need to stop your ear;
Let those who held you captive
Turn pale at the wind's career.
They blow like birds of passage,
And greet you on their way.
With joy they'll bear your message,
For you are the Lord of the day.

What tidings shall you teach them,
What changes shall you choose?
Let psalms of freedom reach them:
Let peace be the world's good news!
The rays of dawn are bursting
Like fountains through the skies;
Oh brother long a-thirsting,
Drink deep of the dawn and rise!

Aaron Kramer
USA

God Help Us To Rise Up

God help us
to rise up from our struggle.
Like a tree rises up from the soil.
Our roots reaching down to our trouble,
Our rich, dark dirt of existence.
Finding nourishment deeply
And holding us firmly.
Always connected.
Growing upwards and into the sun.

Michael Leunig
Australia

O God, I'm Told I Must Compete

O God I'm told I must compete!
My neighbour is the one to beat!
O God, I want to be a friend,
on whom my neighbour can depend.

John Hunt
Aotearoa New Zealand

Lord, Liberate Us

Lord, liberate us from the chains of fear;
Lord, free us from the closed circles of discrimination;
Lord, liberate us from the prisons of prejudice;
Lord, free us from the confines of nationalism.
Lord, liberate us from hate and envy, greed and pride.
Lord, free us from hostility and anger, violence and injustice.
Lord, lead us into the way of peace and justice.

John Johansen-Berg
England

Like an Eagle

False ecstasy
    illusion
        seek repose.
Come soar with me
    like an eagle
Restore the harmony
    that is yours
        if only you will be.
Leave the pain, the toil
    strive no more.
Reach out in trust
    with love.
Soul of thine
    Why do you weep,
        hurt and fight?
Fear no more
    Come soar with me
        like an eagle.
Sift through the debris,
    the vile pollution
Break the barrier
    of your destruction.
Sighing soul hide not,
    Fools we may be
        in your narrow vision
but beyond the mask
    is perceived
  life abused, entangled
    in sheer confusion.
Uncoil, unwind
    Reach upward, outward
        like an eagle
Come soar with me
    find your liberation

true ecstasy
no illusion.

Carys Humphreys
Wales/Taiwan

I Cannot Become Identified

I cannot become identified with the poor of this world but I can at least face the challenge of being identified with the struggle of the poor for their liberation. If I accept that challenge then I must face a radical change in my own life.

Austin Smith
England

Well-fed, Well-clothed

Well-fed, well-clothed, we sing our harvest praise.
We have enough to last through many days,
But starving children cry and are not fed;
They and their parents have no daily bread.

Pot-bellied, gaunt, with great dull eyes they stare,
And mirror the completeness of despair.
With matchstick limbs, listless they move about,
Children too weak to play and laugh or shout.

We who have plenty cannot really share
Their suffering, however much we care,
And everything we do, and all we give,
Is not enough, and millions will not live.

We cannot know, but we can sympathise.
Lord, help us bring some light to those sad eyes.
Help us to spread the seeds of hope around,
And teach us how to plant in fertile ground.

Dorothea Sproule
England

Lord, When Did We See You?

I was hungry and starving
and you were full;
Thirsty
and you were watering your garden;
With no road to follow, and without hope,
and you called the police
    and were happy that they took me prisoner;
Barefoot and with ragged clothing,
and you were saying: 'I have nothing to wear,
    tomorrow I will buy something new.'
Sick
and you asked, 'Is it infectious?'
Prisoner,
and you said: 'That is where all those of your class should be.'
Lord, have mercy!

Author Unknown

A World of Difference – Again

Again I've seen
Into 'the world of difference'.

She came in grey thin pieces of cloth
With two children at her side,
Shadows of people;
Pinched old faces
In children's bodies;
Big eyes
– no anger
– no resentment
At our health and plenty;
– just tired acceptance.
Perhaps our eyes echoed
The anger of them!
Stunted growth with thin spindly legs

165

Tried to balance on the scales,
Wobbling like a new-born foal.

This time no car window
Between us
– that other world was standing before me
In bones and flesh.
Food, clothing,
Love and care were prescribed.

Lord,
Is this You standing here?
Is this the opportunity given
To feed and clothe You?
Do I hear you say
'When you do it to the least of these
my children you do it for Me'?

Alison Stedman
England/Bhutan

From the Deep Recesses of Our Souls, We Cry Out ...

Here we are: pastors, mentors, community workers, mothers,
    wives
        thrown into the dark abyss of oppression.
        Despair and loneliness churn within us
            for we are misunderstood,
                marginalised,
                minusculed
        by family, work, church and society.

The formidable walls of patriarchy hem us in,
        making drab and lifeless
        what once was colourful and throbbing.

BUT

166

Let not the pain immobilise us ...
Let not the fear destroy us ...
Let not the lashings drive us to our knees ...

For we have come together to unearth our hurts
That these may become,
To each one of us,
A source of strength and bonding.

We have come to name
That which maims us that,
By naming it, we might control and,
Perhaps,
Dispel it.

We have come to gingerly cradle in our bosoms
The truth and the power
That will free us to make us

>Women of Dignity:
>Women of Courage;
>Women of Love;

That we may stand and struggle
Alongside all those who cry
From the deep recesses of their souls.

Sharon Rose Joy Ruiz-Duremdes
Philippines

Praying for Shoes

Lord, I had coffee and ice cream
walked into the street
to meet a boy with a dream
with no shoes on his feet
with no self-esteem
and with nothing to eat.

Lord, what could I do
    for such a child of the street
    who was created by you
    and dreams of shoes on his feet?
                    Richard Becher
                    England

The Lost Dream

Mama, I can't find my dream
    I had it last night, but now it's gone.
I was all wrapped up
    in a nice clean sheet
    with a pillow for my head
    and a blanket to keep me warm.
I had a bath before bed
    with hot water from a tap,
    but now I can't find my dream
    and I don't know where it's gone.
I have no pillow for my head,
    no blankets to keep me warm
    and no water for a drink
    let alone for a wash.
Mama, I've lost my dream
    and I don't know where it's gone.
It was with me last night
    until I opened my eyes
    and felt my hard wooden bed
    in the cold tin shack
    with a dusty mud floor.
I lost my dream, Mama,
    I don't know where it's gone
    and I don't know where to look.
Perhaps I got it wrong
    and I never should have dreamed
    for dreams are for the rich
    nightmares for the poor.

Dreams have a price
    and I can't afford to pay
    so I've lost my dream, Mama,
    I don't know where it's gone
    and I can't afford to get it back.

Richard Becher
England

Apoi

In a squatter village
in Mak Mandin
sits my home on stilts
– a little, plank house.
I wander along
the narrow, muddy lanes
of my village,
all alone,
in a world of my own.

I am an only child;
my father left us
before I entered this world
– sometimes I wonder
what he was like.
I hardly see my mother;
she cycles away
before the sun rises,
going to the towel factory
where she works.

She toils until the sky darkens;
then she returns, listless,
too tired to talk to me.
She works hard,
but still we don't
have enough money.

169

The factory people
won't pay her more
because she can't read or write.

My house has no tap;
the water we drink
flows through a hose
from my neighbour's house
for half an hour a day.
The mid-afternoon sun blazes
onto our metal roof;
I feel the searing heat;
it is unbearable.

Then it rains;
the clogged drains
spew out ugly brown water.
The flood waters rise,
gushing into my house.
I see the snakes outside;
I'm afraid – God,
why have you forgotten me?

I don't understand why we should suffer,
why we must feel hungry
in a land of plenty;
in the big city of Kuala Lumpur,
everyone is proud
of the Twin Towers
which touch the clouds.
But I am not;
I am sullen and sad.

When I grow up
I want to be a lawyer,
to find proper houses
for the people of my village;

but I'm only twelve now,
no one understands me
I read the scriptures
searching for meaning
in the silence
of my soul.

My God, my God,
lift me from despair
save us
from this wretchedness
I cry to you
all alone
in a world of my own.

Apoi, aged 12, lives at Mak Mandin, the site of one of Malaysia's oldest industrial zones. The large squatter settlement, typical of many throughout the country, where many factory workers live, lies next to the booming industrial area where dozens of factories are mushrooming. The settlements are neglected and lie in stark contrast to the glittering Petronas Twin Towers – the world's largest buildings – in the capital city, Kuala Lumpur.

Anil Netto
Malaysia

The No-childhood Child

Outside the children laugh and play,
I watch them all, I dare not delay,
My master looks at me with hate,
Bonded to him is my fate.

I am weak, my lone heart pleads,
But man of iron was his greed,
I see the wrong around me lies,
There's none to hear my futile cries.

Bowed down by the weight of earning bread,
A man's burden is on my head,
The infamies I daily see,
Where might is right for those like me,

Victim of man's wrath and whines,
The sun for me never shines,
Terrified I sometimes feel,
Death would've been a better deal.

Illiterate, in my under teens,
No joys of school, or friends, or dreams,
A no-childhood child, there's millions like me,
Born under the shadow of poverty.

Alice Saldanha
India

They Put Your Children Away

Dear God,

They have put your children away:

> in mental hospitals,
> in nursing homes,
> in hostels,
> in day centres,
> in sheltered workshops,
> in special schools and
> in death.

They have put your children away:

> because they fear them,
> because they are different,
> because they are a handful,
> because they cost too much,

because they want physical perfection,
because they cannot cope,
because they don't want them,
because they remind them of
their own fears
about life and meaning and death.

Eternal loving mother,

Your children are rejected,
patronised,
segregated,
manipulated,
used,
experimented on,
thrown away,
and killed.

But you are in them,
the same divine Spark
as in everyone.

If we cannot love them,
then how can we ever find you?
Uniting Church in Australia
National Commission for Mission

Children of the Streets

As we celebrate a new era
you sleep in the shades
of your own shadows,
intoxicated – you create your
own little universe
forcefully shutting your minds
from the realities of life.
Windows and doors shut in your faces,

confining you
to your desperate worlds:
cracked heels
        cracked elbows
                cracked lips.
You never think about church –
it is beyond you –
who can blame you
when you can't make sense about God
 – violent as you are
 – angry as you are
 – dislocated and despised
 – confined to self-pity in your violent, angry
and dislocated universe?
Seeing you sends a shudder
of pain and disbelief
through our veins.
We then shut you outside the doors
of our warm houses,
leaving you in the cold,
struggling to free our minds
from thinking about you.
Do not forgive us
when we intentionally forget you
as we bit by bit rebuild
from the remnants of our messed country.
You know what it is like –
together with you we are victims.
As we study, some preparing
to be decision-makers of the future,
your future is eclipsed ...
How crude Apartheid was –
did we remember you
when we forgave them?
Please, dear brothers and sisters

continue haunting us.
Lest we forget.

Nkisheng Mphalele
Natal

God's Economy

A child cries, she feels the cold
that bites into her bones
for winter is on, and young and old
huddle inside their homes.

No cosy home has Nellie,
her clothes are cast off rags
her shelter a little thatched gullie
patched with gunny bags.

Why dear Lord must Nellie suffer
because her father is dead,
her mother too weak to rough the weather
or struggle for food and bed?

Why dear Lord, should so much pain
be borne by the innocent
while stronger people, proud and vain
have so much and aren't content?

Alice Saldanha
India

You Were a Refugee Too

Then Joseph got up, took the child and his mother by night
and went to Egypt and remained there until the death of
Herod.

(Matthew 2:14)

175

Daily we are confronted
with images of human suffering
on a scale that is hard to imagine.
People tortured,
violated,
treated as if they are not human beings
in fear of their lives
forced to flee their homes in fear of their lives.

Jesus, you were once a refugee,
as a child forced to flee.

Be with the persecuted
the displaced
the vulnerable
the ones whose dreams are filled
with frightening memories.

Companion God,
show your church how to be a companion,
to offer friendship
to those who have forgotten what friendship is.

May your church model the openness
love
acceptance
patience
kindness
and inclusiveness
that gives people a taste
of belonging
to your family.

Uniting Church in Australia
National Commission for Mission

Spirit of Life

Greatest spirit of creation that blows where she wills.
In the beginning you created life out of chaos.
You turned hopelessness into a situation of hope,
You created the things that are and made them good.

Spirit of our ancestors you are the source of our being.
You who journeyed with our great ones before you called
them to the abode of the living dead
Intercede for us, forgive us as you did our foreparents.

Spirit of renewal mould us and shape us.
Make us as you wish, not as we wish.
Can a pot say to the potter what are you moulding?
Cleanse us of our pride and sin.

Spirit of rain we thirst for you.
Visit our desert land and let us experience you.
Let our dry land and our dry hearts be nourished by you.
Make our fields green and our hearts kinder.
Make us love you afresh.

Spirit of life disturb our complacent souls.
Enflame our bones and our will
so that we may run like African antelopes
Declaring your transforming word.

Prince Dibeela
Botswana

Underneath the Arches

I, but a lone voice in the wilderness
Of this great affluent world –
A thorn, pricking discomfort into flesh
Clean, well-fed and soft –
Unwilling to be goaded into action

By an uneasy conscience, when I cry your plight.
What though you sleep on cold, damp paving stones
With only cardboard blankets each dark night –
What though you do not choose to join the race
That jostles folk aside who can't compete!
Those who cannot conform; obey the rules,
Fight back with elbow, boot and tongue must fall
Unheeded by the way.
I'll plead your cause,
But, climbing over bodies piling high
And ever higher, will they hear me call?
Or, hearing, will they pause to think of you?
They have no time – they'll turn away –
'The poor are always with us,'
They'll reply.

Joan Gregory
England

We See Many Imprisoned ...

We see many imprisoned behind brick walls
and held in by iron bars
but they are not so hopeless
as those held captive by hate,
those encircled by prejudice
and those in a prison of fear.
Join the company of the Liberator;
walk alongside the one who breaks the barriers of hate;
share the pilgrimage with the Servant who sets free.

John Johansen-Berg
England

A Prayer for Detained Asylum Seekers

Lord Jesus,
You know how it feels to be a refugee;
to be rejected by your own flesh and blood;

to have no voice, no power, no home;
to be misunderstood, not heard.

In your love, Lord, have mercy on those
who turn to us for freedom but find only a prison.

Have mercy also on us, for our failure to love,
and give us the grace and compassion
to care for those whose lives are in danger
and who seek asylum in our land.

Through Jesus Christ our Lord

A Prison Chaplain
England

Restore My Humanity

Lord!
　　Cleanse my heart and make it
　　　　as white as snow.
　　Make my faith
　　　　as firm as mountains.
　　Make my personality
　　　　as beautiful as flowers.
When I fight for the truth
　　　　make me as brave as the lion.
When I suffer for justice
　　　　make me as meek as a lamb.
When I serve the suffering
　　　　make me as patient as the buffalo.
O God!
　　Restore my humanity.

C. M. Kao
Taiwan

Hear the Cry of the Weak

Hear the cry of the weak,
The bruised and the oppressed;
Their need is greater than our want,
Yet still they are distressed.

Hear the grief of the lost,
Look into sullen eyes:
Unhoused, unheard, no vote, no voice:
All gagged by subtle lies.

Hear the call of the Christ:
'They know not what they do'.
He pleads for us, yet we know well
The greed that we pursue.

(Tune: Awareness)

Andrew E. Pratt
England

Houses of Hope

At the House of Hope in Bethlehem
I delight to meet those who serve
as leaders and houseparents alongside the elderly blind
and the young mentally handicapped residents.
Here in the serving is healing and encouragement;
I delight to share in the exuberance of their worship.

In the Home of Hope in Brasov
I delight to see those who serve
as ministers and helpers in the community centre and church
where old and young meet.
Here in the serving they build for the future.
I delight to share in the depth and dignity of their worship.

180

Two homes of hope, in Israel and Romania,
and the common thread is a deep faith
binding together servants and served
in a community of care
in the name of the Servant King.

John Johansen-Berg
England

Liberating One

Free us from all bondage
so that our faith in you
will make us free
to create with courage
a new world –
new societies

Author Unknown
Asia

Rise Up Again

We have come through the night.
Now we stand in the morning light.
Behind us lie tears of pain.
God has spoken: rise up again.

Chorus: Rea go leboga
Rea go leboga
Rea go leboga
Modimo wa rona

(We thank you, our Lord)

Memories always last.
Ours the dignity of the past.
Rebuild wall, rebuild pride,
that faith and hope and love abide.

Voices speak from the grave:
stand up children, be strong, be brave.
Hold today in your hand,
for the future of this land.

(Tune: Maphkela)

Steve de Gruchy
South Africa

Passover People

(Exodus 11—13)

A people packed and ready,
with sandals on their feet,
(prepared for liberation,
not knowing what they'll meet)
sit down and eat together
God's feast for slaves set free;
committing to a journey
whatever it may be.

> All who need releasing,
> must feast with God today,
> but let us eat with sandalled feet,
> to travel on God's way!

Disciples with their Teacher
the night He was betrayed;
a covenant renewal
in bread and wine displayed.
Though they desert and fail Him
and think that all is lost;
Christ sets them free to journey
for He has paid the cost.

A Christian congregation,
a church with table spread,

we come to meet with Jesus
and at His feast be fed.
We come to be replenished,
moved on, revived, made new
to follow where God leads us
each day, our whole life through.
(Tune: Wir pflugen)

John Campbell
England

Fear

At one time
I knew fear
I cried and ran,
and they tortured me
more.

Then, one beat of their stick
against my body
opened my mind to truth.
If I fear them not
they can do nothing to me,
they can take nothing
more from me.

Now I am free
for I fear no more.

Burma Issues Staff
Thailand

Incarcerated

Incarcerated as a punishment,
Knowing I am paying the price
for my actions.

Time to come face to face
with my true self.

For the first time
attending church,
Hearing stories
about Jesus the liberator,
who loves each and all.

Finding behind bars,
freedom from guilt
and forgiveness from God,
knowing I am loved
and loveable.

Looking out from behind the bars,
I see people who think they are free,
Yet are shackled by their love
of status, power and wealth.

When in my cell,
I pray that all
may know the liberty of the children of God
and live in its fullness.

Ann Shepherdson
England

Life in Its Fullness

(Reflections upon a grapefruit tree in a Jamaican churchyard)

And there
in the church year
rests God
beneath the afternoon sun.
Her weary branches bowing,
heavy with fruit.

Proud leaves
photosynthesising freely –
succulent yellow spheres
the fruits of their labour.

Fleshy vessels
for the seeds of succession.
Hanging in hope –
the pamplemousse of new
creation.
(Shouting with ripeness)

And there
in the churchyard
sits God
beneath her tree.
Resplendent in roundness,
her faithful face glowing
in reflection
of conception.
Heavy breasts
singing soft maternal warmth,
tender hands
pressing gently
on her tight bulging belly.
Caressing in hope –
the birth of new creation.
(Humming with joy)

Grapefruit God
Warmth of the womb
Celebration in creation
filling wicker baskets
and wooden cradles.

But there:
the bitter aftertaste

of citric sweetness,
the pain and panic
of lingering labour
lest we forget
those
who have yet to enjoy
your life
in its fullness.
(Crying for liberation).

Edward Cox
England

Home Coming

(Jeremiah 31:1–17)

Here they come!
God's children are coming home.
When God calls the tune
the air vibrates with the song of laughing voices,
and the ground shakes to the beat of dancing feet.

So thank you, God:

For the inclusive love
which cherishes lame and blind:

For the providential love
which quenches thirst and smoothes the road:

For the liberating love
which rescues the oppressed and restores their identity:

For the embracing love
which gathers a people and guards a flock:

For the generous love
which satisfies need with food in abundance:

For the comforting love
which turns mourning to joy and sorrow to gladness.

Now the sound of weeping ceases
and Rachel's cheeks are dry.
God's children are coming home,
and the future resounds with hope.

Peter Trow
England

Give Us a Voice

Give us a voice
and we will cry out.
We will raise our voices to sing
Our feet will dance
Wherever there are signs of life around us.

Give us a voice
and we will sob.
Weeping with your world,
like a child holding a broken treasure,
a child that will not be comforted.

Voices will sing,
shout
whisper
laugh
weep
comfort

Give us a voice to name truth
and expose falsehood

to encourage the downhearted
and confront the powers

Give us a voice that speaks with passion
And a voice full of compassion
A voice that is gentle
And a voice that is angry

When it would be easier to remain silent
Give us a voice that can speak with conviction.

Give us a voice
And we will proclaim the living Christ.

Voices buried deep will shout out.
Voices that have been submerged will emerge.
Voices that have never been heard will be raised.
Even stones will cry out.

Uniting Church in Australia
National Commission for Mission

God Our Liberator

God our Liberator,
who with a strong hand led the people of Israel
out of slavery to freedom;
through the hands of Jesus, your Son,
you healed the sick, releasing them from bondage;
and through the piercing of his hands on the cross,
you brought the world from death to life.
Make us healers too –
healers of one another and healers of the Earth.
Take our hands into yours,
that we may touch all creation with your love.

Kate Compston
England

Exiles and Those of the Diaspora

God of Ours, we know that you do not make exception among persons and that all are welcome at your great festival of love. Therefore, today we intercede for our great ... community* who live in exile and who have experienced in their own flesh the pain of dispersion.

We recognise that we are an immigrant people, a people that has tasted the sadness of abandoning her native soil to project herself into an uncertain future in a new land. We recognise that we are a people who have lived in poverty, have witnessed wars, have felt the terror of political oppression and have suffered the death and disappearance of loved ones. We are that mixed breed born out of conquest and many of our people continue to be victims of contempt, hatred and marginality. Therefore, we cry to you, to you we pray, to you we lift our supplication: Heal our aches and pains. Calm our anxieties. Apply the balm of your Spirit to the wounds in our souls. Give us the nearness of your friendship that it might produce peace, hope and tranquillity within us.

Help us to know with all certainty that we are no longer foreigners but rather that you have bought our citizenship in the most glorious nation. Help us to see our church as that body of new fellow citizens. Help us to love one another and celebrate our diversity of race, nationality, culture and language because diversity is your gift to humanity. Give us the capacity to see you in all the patterns of faces who form our great people who live in the diaspora.

Today we cry to you believing that no border can limit our drawing near to you and that no human law can impede your reception of us. We ask you to gather us under the secure wings of your power so that together we might march to the Promised Land.

* *Insert the name of your own community*

Daisy L. Machado
Cuba

Yard Sale

If I had a yard sale
who would buy my life
all my disappointments
all my misery as a wife?
If I had a yard sale
who would buy my shame?
I'm tired of covering everything up
thinking I'm to blame.
If I had a yard sale
what would be your favourite lie?
I have a lot of them from a father
I think you'd like to buy.

You see I'm getting rid of everything
that has ever made me cry
so I must sell my whole life
and buy a new one before I die.
If I had a yard sale
how much could I get
for a shy lonely girl
who was an outcast with hopes
of being a beautiful pearl?
Or how about my innocence
that was suddenly stolen away?
I was just a child
wanting only to go out to play.
Here you can have this one for free
I won't even make you pay.
If I had a yard sale
would you like to recycle my dreams?
I have a lot of unanswered hopes and prayers
that I can sell it seems.

Insecurities over in this pile
fears are on the table

and then there is my dysfunction
ready, willing and able.
Everything is outside
dumped right there in my yard
so to find something cheap and broken
shouldn't be very hard.

If I had a yard sale
for everyone to see
selling little bits of my past
selling little bits of me
If I had a yard sale
would you stop and want to buy?
Or just walk right past my life
without a smile or a hi.

Sharon Backus
USA

To Be Set Free

(John 8:36)

Lord Jesus, your love and forgiveness free us so that we can
   serve you and humankind.
Free people so that their enthusiasms and talents
their freedom from poverty and riches
can serve you.

Free people from oppressive social structures
abuses of ownership and power
the exploitation of the poor
and injustice.

Free us from selfishness so that we can work for better human
   conditions,
for the growth of knowledge,
the acquisition of culture,

191

esteem for the dignity of others,
and the acknowledgement of supreme values,
of God and faith.

Lord Jesus, enable us to comfort people in sadness and pain
and to share people's joy
and pleasure.

Simone Rakotomavo
Madagascar

The Justice Tree

The justice tree has bloomed
and suffrage is the flower;
the heart of God delights!
the dispossessed have power:
    now for a hundred years
    in law and living deed
    we own a woman's right
    to stand, to vote, to lead.

New generation, bless
our forebears and their pleading
who knocked and asked redress
from doors that stood, unheeding;
    who, powerless, found the power
    to press their birthright's claim,
    who voiceless, found the voice
    to honour women's name.

The vote is ours to cast
or useless in the winning:
the fabric of our life
needs every thread for spinning
    till no one is deprived,
    in what our lives afford,

by skin or tone or tongue,
of status or award.

In Christ, no walls divide,
no barriers of gender:
this franchise is our faith
which we shall not surrender;
for all our land we pray
in aroha* and trust –
emancipate us still
to make our country just!
*Maori word = warmest love

Shirley Erena Murray
Aotearoa New Zealand

The Open Doorway

The closed door locks in our deepest fears.
Shuts out the thief, the maimed, the stranger,
Protects us both from light and danger,
Saves us from the unwelcome guest
Who may demand attention, disturb our rest.
Threaten and claim our most precious lives.
But closed doors seal us in our own tight fists.

Unlock our hearts, draw back the bolts
Roll stones away –
For the open doorway's wide embrace
Welcomes all unafraid and undismayed
and so makes possible movements of grace.

Jyoti Sabi
India

Forgiveness

(based on Luke 4:18, 19)

Spirit of God, announcing good news to the poor, forgive us,
For the times we have failed to speak your truths about
unemployment
Neglecting those whose skills are wasted in our communities
And allowing the powerful to define the status of the
powerless.

Spirit of God, announcing good news to the poor
Heal us all, to announce your good news.

Spirit of God, proclaiming release to the prisoners, forgive us
For the times we have been trapped by our narrow
assumptions about work
Constricting the feelings and hopes of unemployed men and
women
And refusing to live together as interdependent communities.

Spirit of God, proclaiming release to the prisoners
Heal us all, to release your hope.

Spirit of God, recovering sight to the blind, forgive us
For the times we have lost sight of your vision of justice and
peace
Disregarding our responsibility to fairly distribute work and
wealth
And ignoring the dreams of those who already seek to do so.

Spirit of God, recovering sight to the blind
Heal us all, to see your vision.

Spirit of God, letting broken victims go free, forgive us
For the times we have been trapped by complacency or
powerlessness

Limiting your vision for healing within our society
And denying the potential of your grace and renewal.

Spirit of God, letting broken victims go free
Heal us all, to discover your freedom.

Spirit of God, announcing good news to the poor,
proclaiming release to the prisoners
recovering sight to the blind,
letting broken victims go free
accept these and all our prayers
for the sake of your son Jesus Christ.

Margaret Halsey
England

Out of Silence

Voice 1 I am Peter's mother-in-law; nameless,
family relationships kept me silent since he
married her.
Powerless and homeless, entertaining more
visitors,
I dared to take a stand.

Voice 2 I am a woman who bled; nameless,
a haemorrhage kept me silent for twelve years.
Powerless and penniless, in an anonymous
crowd,
I dared to get in touch.

Voice 3 I am Jairus's daughter; nameless,
illness kept me silent all my childhood.
Powerless and vulnerable, in a quiet room,
I dared to sit up.

Voice 4 I am a foreign woman; nameless,
an insult was meant to keep me silent

195

Powerless and marginalised, ignored again,
I dared to answer back.

Voice 1 Family relationships can still be a life sentence.
Let us now name those confined by family ties,
out of silence ...

Voice 2 Long-term illness can still leave people weak and
powerless.
Let us now name powerless people,
out of silence ...

Voice 3 Childhood can still be a time of vulnerability.
Let us now name vulnerable people,
out of silence ...

Voice 4 Speaking out can still be a risky business.
Let us now name those who speak out,
who empower us out of silence ...

Janet Lees
England

I Believe

Voice 1
I believe in the random nature of reality.
It could happen to you,
It did happen to us
I can't blame anyone now,
although I did at first.
Anger burst out of me:
I wanted to stamp on heads.
Now the anger is bottled up
and leaks out when you enquire kindly
'How do you cope?'

Voice 2

I cope by saying
I believe in the random nature of reality.
But I also believe in the 'perfect child'.
I know I said I didn't want him,
but at his birth I welcomed him.
Stretched beyond all limits
I still say 'I want him'
but what I really want is to return from the hell
I have descended into.

Voice 3

Don't sell me traditional formulae.
Ancient creed sticks in my throat.
There's no place for me in your community
and society has turned its back,
glancing only to gawp at the spectacle.
In this bewilderment, clinging to each other
we ache for a window of opportunity,
and pine for a light of hope.

Voices 1, 2 and 3

Choose your words carefully,
When you say 'I believe', I may have to.

All

**I believe, that God is present,
even in the random:
not the goading God of perfection,
but the guarding God of chaos.**

**I believe, that Christ is angry,
whether bottled up or blurted out:
purging temples of all cosiness
and supermarkets of superstition.**

I believe, that the Spirit is wiser
than conventions of stupidity
or definitions of ability.
Renewing dreams and visions with a sparkling eye.

I believe, we're all believers,
thrown together in confusion,
searching high and low for meaning,
hold my hand, we'll keep on dreaming.

Janet Lees
England

To See the Reality

(to be put in one's own context)

God, help us to remember
the peoples of Latin America
that are now in Australia.

People who came long ago
and have forgotten the struggles of their own peoples.

People who came more recently,
expelled or exiled,
fleeing poverty or war,
willingly or not
– and cannot forget those struggles.

People who have just arrived,
without language, friends or direction.

And, especially people who now want to go back,
to war, violence or 'disappearance',
to poverty, unemployment or upheaval
– rather than continue facing

racism, exclusion and hate
in our society and our churches.

God, help us to see this reality around us,
to open our hearts and minds,
to learn from our neighbours
and to act for justice.

Raúl Fernández-Calienes
Cuba

A Patchwork Prayer

With fragments of hope,
scraps of courage,
gathered together
in your township co-operative,
you celebrate your creativity and skill,
my Soweto sisters.

With dignified calm
and quiet strength,
at your exhibition
to fat white women in hats and gloves,
you tolerate their quibbling over price and style,
my stout-hearted sisters.

With powerful speech,
needle pointed,
boldly straight stitched,
in your well applied exegesis,
you fray the edges of their flimsy arguments,
my word-sewing sisters.

Christ of the seamless robe
and carefully selected patch,
help South Africa to unpick
the cast-off garments

of black servitude
and white oppression,
cutting through the fabric
of a once monochrome society,
piecing together
with faith's invisible thread,
swatches of colour,
ribbons of peace,
till all the children of Leah and Zilpah,
Bilhah and Rachel
wear their technicolour dreamcoats
with equality and pride.

Jean Mortimer
England

Is There Any Hope?

Bangladesh society does not recognise prostitution and
fanatics set fire to their colonies. Amena is twenty-six. Her
mother died when she was very young. Her father is a road-
side vendor and the family live in a village near Dhaka. There
were already six children when her father remarried and then
the family increased to thirteen. After the arrival of a new
mother there was little peace and love in the family but the
young ones tried to stick together and enjoy each other's
company. On returning from school one day, when she was
twelve years old, Amena could not find her elder sister
Ayesha. She learned from the neighbours that Ayesha had
been sold to someone and that she would soon be sold by her
stepmother. She was very afraid so she escaped from the
village and went to Dhaka to find a future.

Amena managed to find a house-maid's job with a well-to-do
family. One day, in the absence of the mistress, the master
approached her with evil motives but she managed to escape.
Amena left and settled down with another family where she
fell in love with a young man. He, with his friends, raped her

one night. She was taken to a hospital to recover. Amena returned to her village home only to be abused and insulted. Later, she returned to Dhaka where she got a small loan from a lady in a red-light district but she could not pay it back and was forced into prostitution. A rickshaw-puller married her and they have a young daughter. However, the husband married a second woman and he wanted them both to earn money for him through prostitution which is something Amena hates. Where is the way out in a society that does not recognise prostitutes exist? How can Amena bring up her daughter in the mess she experiences in her life? Is there any hope for better days for her daughter?

Bishop B. D. Mondal
Bangladesh

Prayer of Life

My Lord, I do not know how to pray. I am illiterate.
No one thought it necessary for me to have education.
Sharing with you joys and sorrows
is a great source of strength and comfort.
I am a product of poor parents, poor environment
but this need not worry anyone
as I have learned to live with realities.
Somehow I have grown up and you have blessed me
with several children.
I live in a slum, no work, no food, no clothing.
I try to work as a contract labourer.
Five rupees a day.
Hardly get one week's work in a month.
Hire and fire is the law of the game.
How can one survive with a family with so limited
resources and with so much insecurity?
Someone advised why not start a self-employment scheme,
government, banks and voluntary agencies help with a loan.
They have good schemes, good plans.
On contacting them I realised

they help people of repute and with good connections.
So, I cannot fit into their schemes.

Sudhakar S. Ramteke
India

Winter

God, God,
today the sun did not rise
on the landscape of my heart.
There is nothing but darkness
nothing to feel but a cold
that goes as deep as my bones.

I am like a bare tree standing alone
amongst the dead leaves of memory.
Storms of grief and anger beat against me
and there is nothing to shelter me.

Why did this happen?

I did not ask for winter.
It came suddenly, beyond my control,
stripping away my comfort
and leaving me desolate and helpless.

It hurts to think.
It hurts to be.

I know that I can't turn back the seasons.
Never again, will I enjoy this last summer,
but in the deep cold of frozen sap,
there is a message of a spring to come
and already, where old leaves fell,
there are the beginnings of new buds.

All I can do today, is lie still and wait,
knowing that when the greenness and light
come again, I will be bigger and stronger
than I was last year.

Joy Cowley
Aotearoa New Zealand

A Teardrop Falls

From the heart of the dove a teardrop falls;
In the heart of the nation not a flutter at all.

A raindrop hangs from the window-sill corner;
Over the mountain the river runs free.

The eye opens wide; fright or excitement?
The goose gently smiles at the wonder of life.

On coastal plain now shackled and tamed;
The relentless march of the city rolls on.

My spirit soars in dreams and in visions;
My feet are tied to this place and this time.

Craig Muir
England

Come and Sit with the Carpenter

Come and sit with the carpenter,
Share with him at the workbench.
He has turned hope on the lathe of love,
Joined heaven and earth with nails,
Planed smooth the splintered creation.

Impaled on thorns of hate
He draws the sting of our despair

And as we plait for him a crown
He carves the throne we're called to share.

See!
He is building a cross,
As a place for healing!
Here the final piece of eternal promise
Is hammered home with bleeding hands.

Come and sit with the carpenter
Share with him at his workbench,
Through toil which costs his life and blood
It becomes a table where all have room
To sit and eat the feast of heaven.

Peter Trow
England

New Wine under the Skin

'When it comes down to it,
the wineskins must change.'

Much as I know I do the right thing,
politically correct,
acceptable and christian,
whenever I ask, all you say is:
'When it comes down to it,
the wineskins must change.'

Of course I'm concerned.
I ponder on famine whilst munching my toast.
I muse about poverty whilst watching TV.
And every night I get on my knees
and ask why you do nothing.
'When it comes down to it
the wineskins must change.'

204

How can you say that?
Must they do it themselves?
They need your wine now:
the refreshment of ministering care
breaking over their pain,
like vino across parched lips.
Lord, what is holding you back?
'When it comes down to it,
the wineskins must change.'

Then I pause, as if a ghost has skipped past my vision.
What if ... ?
And I get down on my knees,
inside and out ...
Lord, I didn't think.
I thought I was moving in step:
the correct words, right thoughts.
'When it comes down to it
the wineskins must change.'

Only new wineskins can refresh the thirsty.
Old wineskins burst and need renewing.
Lord, help me,
I didn't realise ...
That old wineskin is me!

Duncan Tuck
England

And the Bread and Fish Continue To Multiply ...

packets of peace seeds
cornflower blue
sold for peace education
grown to show
that peace is a living bounty
multiplying

    in fertile ground
a sowing of love for our Seed-Maker God.

boilings of marmalade
by cash-strapped old lady
from Citrus-Coast country.
many boilings and more, yet more
sold to boost church building fund
where sweet-sharp christian life bubbled.
a golden boiling for our Golden Citrus God.

flowers from a hundred gardens
gathered by hand
given to volunteer posy-makers
to express Christmas love
for the immobile and shrunken
of body and spirit
who receive the nose-gays
with glowing smiles.
a harvest of love for our Gardener God.

koha-gift of food, money
from all-comers' pocket, purse,
pantry, picking place
to feed and accommodate
the multitude
of mourners on marae
for maori tangi
an ingathering of love for our Rangitira God.

scrap wool knitted steadily by wobbly old fingers
creating bright toys to sell
to help supply the multitude needs
of the multiple needy.
homely work from the leftover pile
bringing simple income, simple outcome of delight

and support.
an intertwining of love for our Weaver God.

the ordinary, the small
made holy, made miraculous
in multiplications
of love
revealing connections of the earthly
and the heavenly
as humble resources are stretched, scattered and amplified
evidence for the naturalness of God's Realm.

Glenn Jetta Barclay
Aotearoa New Zealand

On the Wings of an Eagle

I want to be lifted up and carried away
    on the wings of an eagle.

I want to be able to look down and see the futility of life
    from the heights of freedom and endless space.

Just to know that life doesn't have to be that way.
    That in life there are choices,
        the choice to conform or
    the choice to move beyond conformity.

To be able to continue to walk,
    to soar through life chopping
and hacking away at virgin bush ...
making and discovering the roads
    that have yet to be trodden.

Risking the darkness and danger of wild terrain.
    To move beyond the desire to Retreat,
    to return to old ways and boring routine.

To be happy to discover whatever there is to discover.
   To keep moving forward,
hoping, praying for a new sense of Peace,
a new easier pathway ... yet not complaining,
continuing to accept God's sense of direction,
   even down the deepest of ravines,

trusting and knowing that life can only be lived when one
   learns
   to risk everything, including their life,
in order to discover the beauty that comes,
the honesty that comes from being totally vulnerable.

It's fine, these pathways are so risky,
God would never leave us on our own,
   all alone.
This is Godspace, Godzone
Just let go, allow yourself to be ...
   to become ...

Feiloaigia Taule'ale'ausumai
Aotearoa New Zealand

The Struggle To Be

God you have created us to be us
Yet we have succumbed to be something else.
We have accepted to be surrogate children
of western lifestyles and cultures.
Help us to claim back our dignity as your people.

You have made us black yet we would rather be white.
You have given us beautiful languages but we would rather
take pride in a language of our enslavement.
How can we sing you a new song in a language we can
hardly comprehend?

You taught us that to be is to belong to you
and to one another and to the environment
but we rather listen to our human masters who say,
'To be is to accumulate wealth at all costs.'
Teach us to re-learn our lifestyle of botho*.

Lord we confess our split-personality to you.
We have accepted the fallacy that your worship
is incompatible to our way of life as your people.
Help us to be ourselves, to render unto you worship
full of African fragrance and authenticity.

*This is a setswana word for humanness. It denotes that all people
are inter-related and should therefore live for one another.

Prince Dibeela
Botswana

The Diary

Dates and times;
Appointments to be kept;
Meetings to attend;
Anniversaries to remember;
All tightly scheduled
To fill the day.
The diary tells it all.
It tells of how we use our time,
Of how we fill the hours
And wish we had some more.
Hardly a moment to ourselves;
Almost always under pressure;
Often we drive too fast.
We feel that we are caught –
Held imprisoned
In the little pages
Of our life's day.

Lord,
Set us free within the daily round;
Free to do our work
Without a sense of burden
Or of constant rush and pressure
To get done.
Set us free to live our life
With joy and gladness
In the knowledge of your presence
Everywhere we go.

Robert McN. Samson
South Africa

Servant Song

Poor quality wine it was anyway,
probably poured away by many,
but who were we to question the master.

Filling those jars with water
was no joke.
It seemed pointless.

Feet aching and weary, worn by days of service
then sent to the well –
wedding madness.

For what purpose, a fool's errand completed out of obedience,
but who were we to question the master.

And who was he
who asked for water;
how did he change it?

It was my back that broke
as we trampled the dust
dripping and splashing,

210

wasting our time;
at least that's what it felt like.

Water never tasted so good
and there was enough
even to quench the dust
in my throat;
there was enough to take
away the pain of the task
and bring to our faces
a smile.

Whoever he is I'd like him
to be my master;
at least he knows his wine.

Valerie Shedden
England

Conversion To Christo-centric Life

For the last 2000 years christians have been preaching to people of other faiths to convert from their religion to christianity. Today, the church has to preach to her own members to convert from blind and nominal religious life to a true christian life visible in Christ. One of the oft quoted comments in christian circles today is 'Christlessness' in christian people and their activities. If anyone says he is a christian he should be a follower of Christ which means he is a pragmatic follower. Following Christ does not only mean praying for long hours, reading the bible and attending worship services. Christ stands for love, justice, equality of genders, peace, forgiveness and fraternity of all people. Therefore, believers and followers of Christ should live out the values for which Jesus stood. It is only in Jesus' way we can call ourselves christians when living a Christo-centric life. The fruits of Christo-centric life are harmony and the happy living of all people in this God-created world.

Jeevan Babu
India

Break the Chain

(Matthew 5:38–42, Romans 12:14–21)

The threads of our living,
the joys and the sorrows,
are woven together as one.
A tapestry picture
of all of the feelings
experienced under the sun.
A mix of emotions
and colours of moments,
the canvas is varied and full:
and blame for misfortune
is fickle and foreign
and fuels the divisions that rule.

Break the chain, break the chain,
Linking lives to sadness, break the chain.

Shatter the despair of
cycles of conflict
besetting all humankind:
Gandhi was right when
he said that an eye for an eye
leaves the whole world blind.
Revenge is a rhythm
repeating its sadness
perpetual effect of the past:
justice and peace can seem
simply ideals we desire
to say we hold fast.

Break the chain, break the chain,
Linking lives to sadness, break the chain.

Never give in,
there is hope to be won,
for our future will grow from the seeds.
Kipling can still
come alive for us now
If we keep a firm hold of our heads.
There's always a way
when the will is prepared
to deny the desires that divide,
and truth is released
from its bonds of enslavement
that justify each warring side.

Break the chain, break the chain,
Linking lives to sadness, break the chain.

Stephen Brown
England

A People's Lamentation on Human Rights Day

How long, O Lord,
how long will the peasants remain landless
will the workers remain displaced
will the urban poor remain homeless
will the youth and students remain unchallenged and
    unschooled
will the national minorities remain ostracised and excluded
will the women remain doubly burdened
will the poor remain poor?

How long, O Lord,
how long will the country be governed by manipulative,
exploitative,

and insensitive men
with warped military and capitalist ideologies?

How long, O Lord,
how long will those who hold the reins of government
be beholden
to monopoly capitalism in the midst
of the rising crescendo
of the people's painful and anguished cries?

How long, O Lord, how long
will the power hungry and profit oriented ruling elite
continue to perpetuate the state of affairs
through every conceivable gimmick
Charter Change
People's Initiative,
Party Switching
in a frustrated last ditch
to push the regime's pro-Imperialist and anti-people agenda?

Sharon Rose Joy Ruiz-Duremdes
Philippines

Litany of Commitment

Leader Moses said to the people, 'I call heaven and earth to witness against you this day, that I have set before you life and death, blessing and curse; therefore choose life, that you and your descendants may live, loving the Lord God, obeying God's voice and cleaving to God.'

All In this world
we have the power to choose.
God asks us
to walk the path
of peace, joy and freedom;
to choose life, not death.

214

Men We choose to work for the healing
of our broken world.

Women We choose to forgive our enemies
even as we struggle against them.

Men We choose to take responsibility
for our own and our people's histories.

Women We choose to make amends
where we have been at fault.

Men We choose to treat all people
with equal respect and dignity.

Women We choose to stand firm
against all forms of discrimination.

Men We choose to cry out
against exploitation.

Women We choose to listen to
the voice of the humble.

Men We choose to renounce
all forms of violence.

Women We choose to seek peace
in peaceful ways.

Men We choose to care for the earth
and all living creatures.

Women We choose to live simply
using only what we need.

All	We choose to love and serve
	God and our neighbour
	as Jesus loved and served
	through his death and resurrection.
	In the Spirit's power
	we choose life
	today, tomorrow and forever.

National Christian Council
Japan

Anzac Dawn

Christ of peace
    Prince of peace
        Giver of peace – we pray for peace.
We have had enough of hatred
    which aims a gun at another and pulls the trigger.
We have had enough of resentment
    which destroys by malice or slander.
We have had enough of greed
    which by force or trickery takes what is not rightfully
        theirs.
We have had enough of fear
    which makes children hide lest evil strikes them.
We have had enough of anger
    which explodes to shatter joy.
We have had enough of jealousy
    which denigrates the grace it envies.
We have had enough of memories
    which embitter and feed the evil of our souls.
We have had enough of ancient divisions
    which old people enshrine and which children imbibe
        with their mother's milk.
We have had enough of power
    which usurps the rights of others,
        and manipulates for its own ends.
We have had enough of injustices

which refuse to be righted.
We have had enough!
Child of peace
    Prince of peace
        Giver of peace – we pray for peace – and let it
          begin with us!

E. Body
Aotearoa New Zealand

In the Heart and in the World

Peace in our hearts, you tell me,
Is the first of our torn world's needs.
Yet, how can our hearts lie quiet
When governments all agree
That trade in the deadliest weapons
Must be fostered from sea to sea.

They tell us employment's at stake
If we don't manufacture those guns,
And those myriad germs and those warheads
That factories turn out by those tons.

But how can our workers have peace in their hearts
When they're making those weapons to kill.
To kill whom? For what crime?
In the end no one wins.
So let's take the mote from our eyes,
Think again: there's yet time.
Peace, be still.

Eve Masterman
Australia

In Remembrance

In remembrance of those
throughout time, all over the world,

217

who have died in war,
we pray urgently today
that children, women and men
may become makers of peace.

We pray for children growing up
in violent surroundings,
or thinking, talking or playing in warlike ways.
God, give to your people a new challenge
new ways in which to test their strength –
in sharing power and risking non-violence.

O God, we pray for:
a new awareness of the battlefield within us;
new ways of channelling aggressive instincts;
new thought-patterns, language and ideas;
a new appreciation of the world as one community;
new methods of dialogue and negotiation;
new attempts to befriend those different from ourselves;
new readiness to forgive and reconcile;
new visions, new love, new hope ...
and a new faith, that the peace that passes understanding
can reach out from within us to embrace the world.

Kate Compston
England

A Song for Peace

What did we do when we wanted corn?
We ploughed and we sowed from early morn.
For our hands were strong and our hearts were young,
And our dream was a-dreaming ages long.

What did we do when we needed a town?
We hammered and we nailed 'till sun went down.
Our hands were strong and our hearts were young,
And our dream was a-dreaming ages long.

What shall we do when it's peace we want?
Far more than a man can build or plant.
We shall gather friends from the South and North
And we'll plough and we'll sow till Peace comes forth.

That's what we'll do when it's Peace we want,
When it's more than a man can build or plant.
We shall plough and sow,
We shall hammer and nail
Through all night and all day till Peace is real.

Aaron Kramer
USA

Healing Peace

O God, you have a parent's love for me.
O God, you feel my pain and weep for me.
O Christ, you faced the crucifixion pain.
O Christ, you faced the worst and overcame.
O Spirit, touch me with your healing peace.
O Spirit, hold me and the pain will ease.

John Hunt
Aotearoa New Zealand

I'm Weary, Lord

I'm weary, Lord.
It's not serving you that saps my energy.
It's the people you've given me to work with.
They're difficult.

It's not having a vision of your mission that's hard Lord,
it's the petty personality conflicts.
Where is the vision
that is big,
at least bigger than our egos,
bigger than the kingdoms we are busily building?

It is here, Lord,
in your body,
that we do the best job of wounding one another.

We find it hard Lord, to name
that here, in your church,
we are the ones who impede your kingdom.

Uniting Church in Australia
National Commission for Mission

Trash and Treasure

God,
it seems that you are in the recycling business,
You always see what is worthy and redeemable.
You never discard this world.
You always see the value of each person.

Like those that scrounge around the tip finding something of
   value,
**You sent Jesus into the world as part of your great saving
   plan.**
Those who were the forgotten ones in his society
He loved.
Those who were placed on the garbage dump
He made new.

God,
you are the great scavenger and
the great conservationist.
Include us in your recycling plan.
Remind us that what the world considers
nonsense, and throws out as weak and useless
Is the most valuable of all.

Uniting Church in Australia
National Commission for Mission

220

Hope

Hope is there
like a smouldering fire
that cannot be extinguished ...
some day that purifying furnace
will heat a decent poor person's stove.

Author Unknown
Haiti

I Am a Woman

I am a woman
    I am alive
        I am struggling
            I am hoping.

I am created in the image of God
just like all other people in the world.
I am a person with worth and dignity.
I am a thinking person, a feeling person, a doing person.
I am the small I am that stands before the big I AM.

I am a worker who is constantly challenged and faced
    with the needs of the Church and society in Asia
    and in the global community.

I am angered by the structures and powers that create
    all forms of oppression, exploitation and degradation.
I am a witness of the moans, tears, banners and
    clenched fists of my people.
I can hear their liberating songs, their hopeful prayers and
decisive
    march towards justice and freedom.

I believe that all of us – women and men,
    young and old, christian and non-christian

221

are called upon to do responsible action;
to be concerned
to be involved
NOW!

Elizabeth Tapia
Philippines

Courage

Do not be afraid of standing up for what you believe; what you do, no matter how small, will make a difference.

> A candle is a protest at midnight.
> It is a non-conformist.
> It says to the darkness,
> 'I beg to differ.'

Indian Proverb

Fear Not

Those in power can no longer overlook the handwriting on
the wall
their subjects think twice about nodding in agreement
the weapon dealers no longer dare to walk over the weak
bishops stop equivocating and say no
the friends of Jesus block the roads of overkill
school children learn the truth.

How are we to recognise an angel
except that he brings courage where fear was
joy where even sadness refused to grow
objections where hard facts used to rule the day
disarmament where terror was a credible deterrent.

Fear not: resistance is growing.

Dorothee Sölle
Germany

Psalm from Prison

From this dark and lonely cell
I cry out to you,
Lord hear my groaning.

I don't know where I am.
I don't know whether it's night or day.
I don't know what will happen next.

My throat is sore, I cannot scream anymore.
My fingers are swollen, I cannot clench my fist.
My ribs are broken, I cannot stand erect.

I hate the sight of water
    I can no longer bear a single drop.
I loathe those cigarettes
    that penetrate my skin.
I dread the sound of footsteps
    and the opening of the door.
I prefer this darkness
    than face the glaring light.
I can just imagine
    what they are going to do next.

They said only I can end my suffering
if I cooperate with them
and sign the confession they manufactured
and bear false witness against myself
and those who oppose this diabolical regime.

How much longer, O Lord, can I hold on?
How much longer can I maintain my sanity?
How long will they keep me in this limbo?

Will I ever see again the sun?
Will I ever see again the faces

of those I love and serve?
Or will they make me disappear forever?

Lord, deliver us from these kidnappers and murderers
    who are trying to maintain peace and order.
Deliver us from these mercenaries
    whose obsession is to defend national security –
the security of this bloodthirsty
    and power-hungry dictator,
the security of his cronies and their
    big business interests,
the security of his alien lords
    and their bases and investments.

O Lord, my God,
I know that you are neither blind nor deaf.
Your mercy and compassion endure forever.
You have always been a subversive God:
    you scatter the proud,
    you depose the mighty,
    you empty the rich,
    you lift up the lowly,
    you free the oppressed,
    you fill the hungry.

I cry out now to you:
    subvert this evil kingdom and empire!
Let your spirit fill the hearts
    of those who are struggling to build your kingdom
    of justice, peace and freedom.

From this dark and lonely cell
I cry out to you, Lord hear my prayer.

Into your hands, O Lord
I commend my broken body
and my wavering spirit.

Amado L. Picardal
Philippines

Conspiracy*

Come, join the conspiracy ...
Together, let's conspire!
Shallow breath,
Caught by twentieth-century air.
The air of twenty centuries, trapped in our lungs.
Tightened chest,
Labouring lungs,
Straining to enlargen.
Narrow constrictions gripping us,
The narrow passageways of half-thought thoughts,
Of half-dreamed dreams, of half-loved loves,
Of half-schemed schemes.
Let go the fortress-held stance of shallowly-breathed patterns.
Breathe deeply now.
Echoes of another call ...
Come and See!
Now ... come and breathe.
Yes! Come join the conspiracy ...
Together, let us conspire!

The Latin root of the word conspiracy means to breathe together.

Margo Ritchie
Canada

Birth Pangs

Lord: Help us to see in the groaning of creation not death but
birth pangs; help us to see in suffering a promise for the
future, because it is a cry against the inhumanity of the
present. Help us to glimpse in protest the dawn of justice, in

225

the cross the pathway to resurrection and in suffering the
seeds of joy.

Rubem Alves
Brazil

'Nobodies' to 'Somebodies'

Lord, help us to link arms with our brothers and sisters who
are forgotten, wherever they may be, knowing that this is the
task of the body of Christ. And in those we meet today, may
we always be sensitive to those whom life seems to push
down. May we remember to be with you in lifting them up –
to let the 'nobodies' be 'somebodies'.

Garth Hewitt
England

God of the Margins

God of the margins, we pray
– for those living on the edge:
the poor, the lonely, the alienated,
the strangers in our midst;
those isolated by mental or physical illness,
by bereavement or family breakdown;
who have crossed frontiers or missed out on education;
those who slip through the net of social caring,
whose voices are unheard,
who are not quite respectable (though worthy of respect)
– for ourselves, that we may learn
from our sisters and brothers
about resilience and hope against the odds,
about celebration and sharing,
that we may never make assumptions,
or make the church exclusive
when God's love includes all.
We pray in the name of Christ, at the heart of all.

Jan Sutch Pickard
England

Circle

Circle-sitting
like a bowl
we held the silence
shared the weight
between us
juggling, balancing
– until it seemed
quite effortless
and feather-light
– until the stillness
was the womb
that cradled us.

Later
the wisdom of the body
knew the moment and
not without pain
the contractions
pushed us away
from our connectedness.
Time to break circle
time to be born
into word and action.
But going with us
stillness within
to make the ordinary shine.
The waters that break
are not lost. They
will be taken up, our days
nourished by them. They will fall
gentle as rain
again, again ...

Kate Compston
England

227

God, You Hold Me Like a Mother

God, you hold me like a mother
Safely on her knee;
God, you hold me like a mother
Close to you but free.

God, you watch me as I wander,
Keep me in your sight.
God, you watch me as I wander
Hold me day and night.

God, you hold me like a mother,
Teach me to be free.
God, you hold me like a mother,
Show your love to me.

(Tune: God, You Hold Me)

Andrew E. Pratt
England

Take Our Hatreds

Take our hatreds:	make them into handshakes
Take our prejudices:	make them into peace-offerings
Take our arguments:	make them into bonds
Take our misunderstandings:	make them into music
Take our divisions:	make them into dances
Take our schisms:	make them into songs.

Kate Compston
England

He Was Laid in a Manger

Out of all the:
beautiful houses
well-to-do families

228

professionals in Bethlehem
families of the Pharisees
beautiful girls in Judea
richest cities in the world.

Jesus was born:
in a cattle shed
to a poor, insignificant but obedient family
to a carpenter named Joseph
and a young woman, Mary
in Bethlehem.

May your Holy Spirit enable us to realise that your birth
indicates that our mission involves working with the:

marginalised
destitute
forgotten
AIDS victims
widows and orphans
and Untouchables;

whatever we do to the least of his brethren.

Goodwin Zainga
Malawi

A Great Country

Lord!
Grant us strength to build
a great country.
where people respect everyone's human dignity,
where people sincerely love the suffering,
where people protect the oppressed,
with righteousness and compassion.

O Lord,
>Enable us to make rivers clean, forests green,
>>skies blue, flowers blossom, birds sing
>>>and all creatures happy.
>Enable us to contribute to the
>>justice, peace and progress of
>>>all human beings.

C. M. Kao
Taiwan

Destruction and Salvation

Storms and earthquakes
>killed many people and
>>destroyed many houses.

Egoism, violence and sexual immorality
>killed more souls and
>>destroyed homes.

But, in Christ
>with faith, wisdom and love
>>you can gain new strength,
>overcome difficulties and sins
>>and lead a victorious life.

C. M. Kao
Taiwan

Encounter at the Well

The story of Jesus and the Samaritan woman has always fascinated me, especially after living for fourteen years in Nablus .... We were an Anglican pastor's family. Every time I entered our church, St Philip's, I read above the altar that verse, imparted to the woman of Samaria during that brief, yet so rich encounter Jesus had with her: 'God is spirit, and they that worship him must worship him in spirit and in truth.'

Nothing short of a complete change in attitude satisfied him. It was not so-called 'holy places' he cared for. It was people and their attitude towards God and each other that concerned him, for when that is correct, everything else falls into place.

Our time in Nablus was a very challenging one. It was there that I learnt what it was like to feel my knees turn to water at the sound of Israeli soldiers' boots on our doorstep, or my mouth go dry as they searched the house for I never knew what. It was there that the term 'tongue-tied' became real and I thought my twelve-year-old daughter would never speak again. It was there that we saw our teenage son completely broken, unable to take any more and seeking release from life. It was there that I stood shivering alongside my neighbour, as she first laid eyes on the bullet-ridden body of her seventeen-year-old daughter and I tried in vain to comfort her. It was in Nablus that we, as a family, wrestled with our faith. We tried to pull ourselves through and help others along the way .... There was a conflict raging inside me between the Palestinian, the Christian and the woman.

But through the mediation of the gospel, my peace process had begun. The tripartite meeting took place; peace and harmony won, and a Palestinian Christian woman became one whole person.

Cedar Duaybis
A Palestinian Episcopalian

When Our Culture or Religion

When our culture or religion
Blinds us to complicity
In the systems of oppression,
Bring us love to set us free;

Turn our hearts and minds away from
Intrigue and duplicity,

231

Then from systems that enslave us,
Lord, bring lasting liberty.

Fire a mood of coexistence,
End repression, set lives free,
Break the bonds of hidden hatred,
Lord forgive ... begin with me!
(Tune: Reydon or Love Divine)

Andrew E. Pratt
England

Free Treasure

Go, knowing that you possess the greatest of treasures,
not because you earned it, but because it was freely given.
Go into this world, giving it freely to all you meet,
knowing that the more you give it away
the more it grows in value for you.
Give them God, revealed in Jesus Christ,
made ours by the Holy Spirit.
In the name of the Trinity of love.

Duncan Tuck
England

The Two Brothers

Once there were two brothers. Together they owned one field.
Each of them received half the yield of the field. Harvest-time
came.

After having worked hard during the day, both of them were
very tired and went to bed. The elder brother could not get to
sleep. He thought: 'It's not fair if I receive half the yield, for I
live alone and my brother has to provide for his wife and
children.'

So he got up, went to his part of the field, took three sheaves
and put them beside those of his brother.

The younger brother could not get to sleep. He thought: 'It's not fair if I take half the yield. My brother is unmarried, he needs an extra portion to be able to save for his old age, while my children will take care of me.'

So he got up, went to his part of the field, took three sheaves and put them beside those of his brother.

In the morning when they arrived in the field, they were surprised since each of them had still the same number of sheaves but they didn't say anything. On the second night each brother again added three sheaves to those of his brother. The next morning they saw that nothing had been changed. Again, they were surprised, but didn't say anything.

On the third night, when they were moving the sheaves, they met in the middle of the field. At that moment they understood what had happened. They embraced and wept. Jews assert that on that place, Jerusalem, the city of peace, was built.

Bart Baak
The Netherlands/Bangladesh

Shared Blessings

As you continue on your way,
may you know that God is there.
By the strength of His Spirit,
share your faith with the uncertain;
share your love with the unloved;
share your presence with the lonely.
And share God with everyone,
just as God has shared all with you,
in the unfading blessing of Jesus Christ.

Duncan Tuck
England

Prayers of Touching

(Matthew 25:31–46)
(to be used separately or corporately, concluding with
'We ask in the name and for the sake of Jesus Christ')

Creator God

Creator God,
>   incarnate in Christ our Lord,
>   present in your Spirit, we hear your summons to care for
>   the lost, for the unloved, for those in pain or disgrace ...
>   ... that through even us your healing grace may touch lives
>   caught in despair.

Loving God

Loving God,
>   friend of outcast and stranger,
>   prejudiced in favour of those whom others reject, we ask
>   your blessing on those banished to the periphery of
>   community – detached and alone, feeling worthless and of
>   no value ...
>   ... that their lives be touched with the knowledge that you
>   number the hairs on their heads, and love them whole-
>   heartedly.

Gracious God

Gracious God,
>   We rejoice that you are to us Father and Mother
>   and that we know ourselves gathered up into the family
>   and household of the church – brother and sister pilgrims.
>   All the more, then, do we keenly feel for those for whom
>   the very word 'family' brings pain and regret.

>   And so we pray for those who feel loss or guilt or shame or
>   defilement or neglect or despair in family life ...

... that the church as family stands as a sign of forgiveness and renewal, healing and joy – touching tainted family lives with new hope.

Living God

Living God,
  we pray for all whose living is hard:
  those caught in confusion, those debilitated by doubt, those exploited in the tarnished name of love, those enduring the emptiness of isolation, those tortured by guilt, those fearing to face change ...
  ... that these hard lives all be touched by the transforming grace of your loving presence.

BUT it is not enough, Lord God, that we pray for all these; but that we pray too for ourselves – that we who voice our concerns for others find words of hope and renewal to speak to them, we who agonise over their circumstances find actions that channel your grace to them ...
  ... guide us, we pray, to begin to be – as you will – the answer to the prayers we offer, that lives be touched and transformed and made whole, with hope reborn.

We ask in the name and for the sake of Jesus Christ.

Stephen Brown
England

A Prayer for a Party

  Loving God – if you were present among us now,
  you would be singing and dancing
  and swaying and smiling
  and waving your flag as high as you could –
  for you are a God who loves partying.

235

You are a God of fun and laughter
  as well as of serious talk;
You are a God of dancing in the aisles
  as well as of the sedate walk;
You are a God of rip-roaring song
 as well as of quiet, stillness, silence.

When our lives are humourless – forgive us;
When we avoid eye-contact with our friends – forgive us;
When we are too preoccupied to smile – forgive us;
When we become cynical about laughter and having fun and
  dancing,
forgive us and set us free to laugh at ourselves.

Ruth Harvey
England

We Have No King but Caesar

(John 19:1–30)

You see how I vacillate Lord
when my life is in danger.

I should be shouting 'Away with Caesar!'
You know how I hate the presence of these overlords,
who bring their foreign culture,
who militarise our streets,
who make us feel so inferior.
But when I'm threatened,
I must side-step the truth.
I must chant and dance with the crowd
'We have no King but Caesar.'

If I declared myself openly for you Lord,
what would it mean?
Down which insecure alley will you lead me?

I see the Caspirs in the street,
the crowd moving away from me.
I see the inside of a courtroom,
the place of execution,
the loneliness of a person on his way to the cross.
And I don't want to share that loneliness.

In the business meeting,
the student controversy,
the family discussion,
the ratepayers' gathering,
the classroom decision.

I move to the crowd, and cry ...
'We have no King but Caesar.'

Bob Commin
South Africa

At Home in the City

(Jeremiah 29:1–9)

A place of fear, a place of joy –
a city can be both,
we can allow it to destroy
our hope, our joy, our worth;
like exiles sink into despair –
blaming God for it all
or pray and work with those who care –
responding to God's call.

So let us pray with all our hearts
for those who suffer here:
the disillusioned, unemployed
and those who're trapped by fear.
Cry out for opportunity,
confidence (true and strong):

that God may act through people's lives
to right our city's wrong.

And let us work to strengthen joy
– create community –
that hope and laughter may break out
as people are set free!
For none are free if some are trapped;
none of us stands alone.
God, use us for our city's good,
'til all can call it home.

(Tune: Kingsfold)

John Campbell
England

Celtic Blessing

Be still
And let God's peace wash over you
Like waves lapping over pebbles
Smoothing rough edges of insurmountable worries
To tiny insignificant grains of sand,
Taking away the jaggedness of sin
To leave smooth shining love.
And let the peace of God,
The Father, Son and Holy Spirit
Be with us all today and every day.

Lesley Steel
Scotland

God Help Us if Our World Should Grow Dark

God help us
If our world should grow dark;
And there is no way of seeing or knowing.
Grant us courage and trust
To touch and be touched

To find our way onwards
By feeling.

Michael Leunig
Australia

Dance and Sing

(Based on Exodus 15:20–1)

Miriam, our sister from ancient times,
We find it hard to let ourselves go;
To abandon ourselves to sheer joy;
To get carried away.

We have forgotten how to dance and shout.
We are too world weary.
The victory you experienced,
Seems far removed from our world.
The chariots that destroy and demean
are out in force trampling on the poor.
And the longed for waters that will gush forth, carrying them
away,
seem to have dried up.

Miriam, show us how to discern the signs of life around us;
To proclaim the possibility of freedom from oppression.
Help us to discover that even now –
God is dancing with us,
A dance of hope and joy;
A dance of resilience and resistance.
Then we will take up our tambourines and join you.
Voices buried deep will shout out.
Song will burst forth
And our feet will dance.

Helen Richmond
Australia

Glimpsing the Kingdom

What a Joyful Celebration

What a joyful celebration
when we come together
as a community of communities,
a network of worshippers with common purpose,
a united walk towards the promised land.
Jesus goes ahead of us
as the shepherd leads the sheep
and we hear the song of the redeemed
as prisoners are released, the blind given sight,
the exploited and oppressed are given new hope
and the rainbow sign arcs above the pilgrims
who walk together to the city of peace.

John Johansen-Berg
England

To Christ Our Creator

For poetry, and scholarship and art,
For music's glorious cadences of sound,
For colour, light, and home's alluring hearth,
For beauty's shining traces which abound.
We offer to our great Creator praise,
And bless Him for the wisdom of His ways.

For food and warmth and every kind of skill,
For work, and energy to serve and care,
For thought, and plan, design, and strength of will,
For every noble attribute we share,
We offer to our great Creator praise,
And bless Him for the wisdom of His ways.

For every facet of the Christian faith,
For Christ, supreme inspirer of our hope,
For His true universal church of grace,
For all the members who enjoy its scope,
We offer to our great Creator praise,
And bless Him for the wisdom of His ways.

For peace of mind and happiness of heart,
For concord, judgement and humility,
For every flowing, curving, shape and craft,
For sight and touch, humour and harmony,
We offer to our great Creator praise,
And bless Him for the wisdom of His ways.

Gwendoline Keevill
England

Weaver of the World

Creator God,
weaver of the world in all its variety,
you know our warp and weft: where we cross,
the diverse colours of our opinion, the textures of
    our faith,
you feel our quality,
you touch our frayed edges,
you accept us:
you love us, different as we are –
Thank you.

Christ of the seamless robe,
again and again we strip you
and cast lots, arguing over material things,
missing the meaning of ministry,
averting our eyes from the cross,
failing to be your Body in the world –
Forgive us.

Holy Spirit, networking in the church,
forming our loose ends into a fishing net,
where the strands hold hands around the holes,
making our daily work a sign of God's work in the world,
sign of our connectedness,
sign of our calling:
help us to hold together
and to draw others into your kingdom –
Use us.

Jan Sutch Pickard
England

The Whole Creation

(Based on Mark 16:15; Romans 8:18–23; Colossians 1:15–20
and Revelation 21:1, 3–6)

All-embracing God,
we thank you that your good news –
that life conquers death
and faith overcomes fear –
is for the whole creation,
and not for humankind alone.

We thank you that the universe itself –
suffering now as if in the pangs of childbirth –
waits with us, in eager expectation of deliverance,
and looks forward to a new freedom
from pain and frustration,
torture and abuse.

We thank you that your promise to reconcile
the whole cosmos to yourself
began to be realised in the self-giving of Christ,
whose cross stretches from earth to heaven,
gathering up the wounds of the universe
and offering them as harbingers of the resurrection.

245

We thank you for the shining dream
of a new heaven and a new earth,
where you will be seen at last
as undergirding, permeating and transforming all things.
In the light of that vision, may we live together now
with hospitality and gentleness, longing and love.

Kate Compston
England

Bringing Harmony

God of the green pastures and still waters,
help my heart to beat in time
with the quiet music of your creation.

The National Society
England

In the End — a New Beginning

spirit of new beginnings,
when our plans crack and crumble;
when we board up our hopes
    and abandon our dreams;
when our future
    is ravaged by unforeseen changes
    or vandalised by other agendas
when the confidence
    we had in the beginning
    is shaken to the ground;
when all is in ruins
    and all seems ended ...

show us, holy spirit,
in broken wall and opened roof,
    where stones rolled away
    let in your light
    and breath;

show us where
>your rising vine is greening
>**to create — in the end —
>a new beginning.**

Norm S. D. Esdon
Canada

Perspective

The Spirit knitted
my frayed hopes
and in a moment
set me on a high
but lowly place.

I saw the whole majesty
of the human story
unfolding before me,
from the first wanderings
to Mother Teresa's smile.

Abraham and Sarah passed by,
Nefertiti flowered and died,
Homer recited his verse,
Rome marched triumphant,
and Light exploded in Bethlehem.

John wrote his gospel,
Francis and Clare led the poor,
Leonardo painted Mona Lisa,
Mozart eavesdropped on heaven,
Einstein deciphered a mystery.

In one moment of sight
I beheld your glory,
the unlikely splendour

shining wondrously
from one small planet's dust.

Yet it was all contained
easily in one drop of dew
on one needle of one sheoak,
caught briefly in the light
of the rising sun.

Bruce D. Prewer
Australia

A Litany for Urban Ministry

*(Responses to be said by all are in **bold** type)*

O God who hurts when we hurt and suffers when we suffer,
we pray for city communities where hope is often scarce, self-
esteem sorely pressed and fear and mistrust a part of daily life
for many. Great God we pray –
 **– for the building of your Kingdom in damaged city
 communities.**

O God who cares for the whole of each of us, we pray for every
effort to show Your care – through lunch clubs, youth clubs,
friendship support in building community and help to heal
the hurts of body, mind and soul. Great God we pray –
 **– for all who share in living out Your care for whole
 persons.**

O God who calls us to be one people in Your name, we pray
for every effort that enables all Your people to stand together
as one. Great God we pray –
 **– for the common witness of all Your people to our one
 Saviour.**

248

O God who uses imperfect, fragile people to carry the treasure of Your presence to others, we pray for all our sisters and brothers who carry on trying to care, in Your name, even when they themselves hurt. Great God we pray –
 – **for fragile saints who offer themselves in Your service.**

O God who is 'not far from any one of us', we pray for humble listening and learning and gracious sharing of the truths we think we know, when we meet people of other faiths or no faith. Great God we pray –
 – **for our part of the search for truth in the midst of many faiths.**

O God who for us faced every evil and overcame them in the struggle, we pray for those who daily face evils such as racism, or violence, or poverty yet still retain their dignity and continue to live with hope. Great God we pray –
 – **for all whose lives are blighted by evil.**

O God who calls us to be part of one caring, helping family, we pray for those who minister on behalf of us all in pressured urban communities. Great God –
 – **we offer now our full support for this urban part of our shared ministry.**

In the Name of our Saviour Jesus Christ.

John Campbell
England

A Litany on Community Sharing

Leader 1 (a woman) People of God, let us come together in the presence of God and in the presence of each other. God is here. We are here, so let us celebrate!

249

People	Yes, we celebrate being here and we celebrate being alive. Now is the time to commune. Now is the time to live as a community.
Leader 2 (a young male)	How do we live as a community? Do we really share as a community? Who is in and who is out? Maybe we need to confess before we affirm something. Do you hear me?
People	Yes, we hear you. Your probing questions make us think. We confess to God we think of community but we are afraid to live as a community. May God forgive our indifference and prejudices.
Leader 1	God forgives our sins. As a sign of change of heart, we will need to change our ways. What are the ways we can change?
Youth	Begin to listen to us, and give us room to grow and to question.
Women	Let go of the power to control and to exploit. Listen to our voices. Be enriched by our gifts.
Senior Folks	Our bodies might be weak but count us in. Our experiences are not the same but we can still share.
Men	We pledge to listen more and to work with others in the spirit of love and communal sharing.
Leader 2	Now we are coming together, listening to each other, learning from one another. May God bless our journeying together, practising the kingdom of God in this

place, venturing into communal learning and sharing. Praise be to God!

People   Praise God who calls us into being!
Praise Jesus Christ who calls us into
   living!
Praise the Spirit who calls us into
   loving!

Elizabeth Tapia
Philippines

Invited Guests

(Luke 14:15–24)

The feast was spread for all to see,
the host then summoned company;
successful, rich and satisfied
they made excuses – even lied.
   Lives filled with self, lives packed with pride
   – lives too full to let God inside!

The host then sent to scour each street
for those whom 'nice' folk never meet.
He welcomed poor and blind and lame;
those crushed, forgotten, trapped by shame.
   Lives needing healing, lives raw and sore –
   lives our God could make whole once more!

The summons spread across the land,
'til all the hungry were at hand;
the door then closed to leave outside
those rich, complacent, satisfied.
   Feast for the crushed, feast righting wrong
   – feast that shouts God's great justice song!

This feast's now spread for you and me,
if we'll accept God's company.

Christ summons us from near and far,
no matter who or where we are.
      Laid down his life, paid every cost –
      Wine and bread to revive the lost!

So let us come and share what's given –
this foretaste of the feast of heaven –
respond, receive, and be made new
for all the things we're called to do.
      Receive God's gift, that we may all
      live our lives to announce God's call!

(Tune: Sussex Carol)

John Campbell
England

I Believe in God

Voice 1   I believe in God: creator and farmer, lover and friend, challenger and enabler; wellspring and womb of purposeful living.

All   **We believe in God.**

Voice 2   I believe in Jesus Christ: compassionate and wounded healer, wise-one and fool; liberator from oppression.

All   **We believe in Jesus Christ.**

Voice 3   I believe in the Spirit; go-between and negotiator, inspirer and encourager; barrier-breaker, community-maker.

All   **We believe in the Spirit.**

Voice 4   I believe in the community of faith: alive in the aliveness of Christ,

prophetic in its solidarity with all who suffer,
celebratory in its hope, its work, its witness.

All   **We believe in the community of faith.**

Voice 5 I believe in God's kingdom: beckoning and
burgeoning, dynamic and harmonious, present
and future; in which we glimpse
– the satisfaction of our deepest longings
– the healing of our painful rifts
– the forging of justice, peace and integrity.

All   **We believe in God's Kingdom.**

Kate Compston
England

Hispanic Creed

We believe in God, the Father Almighty
Creator of the heavens and the earth;
Creator of all people and all cultures;
Creator of all tongues and races.

We believe in Jesus Christ, his Son, our Lord,
God made flesh in a person for all humanity,
God made flesh in an age for all the ages,
God made flesh in one culture for all cultures,
God made flesh in love and grace for all creation.

We believe in the Holy Spirit
through whom God incarnate in Jesus Christ
makes his presence known in our peoples and our
cultures;
through whom, God Creator of all that exists,
gives us power to become new creatures;
whose infinite gifts make us one people:
the Body of Christ.

253

We believe in the Church
    universal because it is a sign of God's Reign,
    whose faithfulness is shown in its many hues
    where all the colours paint a single landscape,
    where all tongues sing the same praise.

We believe in the reign of God – the day of the Great Fiesta
    when all the colours of creation will form a harmonious
        rainbow,
    when all peoples will join in joyful banquet,
    when all tongues of the universe will sing the same song.

And because we believe, we commit ourselves:
    to believe for those who do not believe,
    to love for those who do not love,
    to dream for those who do not dream,
    until the day when hope becomes reality.

Justo González
Cuba

We Are Here, Lord

Leader   We are here, Lord, because we believe.
            It is your gift and our struggle.
            Help us to free ourselves from all that
            enslaves us.

Response   Lord, set me free.

Leader   We are here, Lord, because we believe in
                justice.
            It is your gift and our struggle.
            Help us to work for justice in our own lives
            in our nation and in the world.

Response   God of justice, lead us on.

Leader	We are here, Lord, because we believe in unity.
	It is your gift and our struggle.
	Help us to build bridges, to reach out in solidarity, in sisterhood and brotherhood.

Response	Lord, make us one.

Leader	We are here, Lord, because we believe in peace.
	It is your gift and our struggle.
	Help us change the injustices and inequalities that destroy true peace.

All	God, of peace, lead us on.

Action for World Development
Australia

The Liturgy of the Tree

This liturgy was written for a Mission Education School in Jamaica. It drew inspiration from a rubber tree, with magnificent air roots, growing in the grounds of the venue, and from Ephesians 3:17. Together these suggested that we might not always think of our prayers as rising to God. God is with us here on earth and we can reach down deep into God's love. Afterwards, prayer cards were tied to the roots of the tree.

In the heat of the day the tree gives shade. Beneath its broad leaves and arching branches we come to take our rest.

With great delight I sat in the shadow of my beloved and the fruit was sweet to my taste.

Song of Solomon 2:3b

In the sweat of labour, may God give rest and food.

Roots stretch down, searching for water, reaching in hope, drawing from deep in the earth refreshment and nurture.

God, you are my God. I seek you, my soul thirsts for you, as in a dry and thirsty land where there is no water.

Psalm 63:1

In the longing for justice and equality, may God give hope.

Wind moves in the branches, leaves stir. The air warm and moist, we feel the invisible power, its gentle strength.

I called on God, and the Spirit of Wisdom came to me. The immortal Spirit is in all things.

Wisdom of Solomon 7:7b, 12:1

In the search for renewal, may God breathe on us with wisdom.

The roots tangle and twist as they extend and push down, holding the tree secure in the earth.

Christ dwells in our hearts through faith as we are being rooted and grounded in love.

Ephesians 3:17

In the places of risk, may God give security and love.

All things living will die. Even in its life, we recognise the tree will not last forever. Yet it promises more, in its fruit and its seeds.

Christ has been raised from the dead, the first fruits of those who have died. What is sown is perishable, what is raised is imperishable.

1 Corinthians 15:20, 42b

For the violence of death, may God give life.

Michael Durber
England

Celebrate All Human Beauty

Celebrate all human beauty
caught in colour, form and face,
celebrate the human body
made to move with speed and grace.
    Celebrate the human spirit
    leaping high to reach a goal,
    celebrate our Maker's wisdom
    crafting body, mind and soul.

Celebrate our own endeavours
to achieve and to arrive
over handicap and hurdle
when against ourselves we strive,
    iron will and summoned courage
    sweeping obstacles aside,
    sweating out our inner conflict
    to acquit ourselves with pride.

Sport and faith both speak a language
universal, sensed and known;
where there's shared exhilaration,
new community is grown,
    friendship found in common focus,
    effort turned to common goal,
    honouring our maker's purpose,
    health in body, mind and soul.

                Shirley Erena Murray
                Aotearoa New Zealand

Not with Voices Only

Not with voices only
we praise you,
Loving God,
but with everything we are:

our whole being,
body, mind and soul.

Your praise
is our health.

When we praise you,
not with hope of reward,
but in the pure joy
of what we already receive;
we are brought
fully to life
by your own Holy Spirit.

When we praise you,
with no thought of self,
but just for sheer delight
that you are
what you are,
we come to life with the resurrected Christ,
and find ourselves
your children,
each one immeasurably loved,
in time and to eternity.

Body, mind and soul
praise you:
and our lives unfold like a rose
in silent praising beauty.

Silence

Be adored, be adored, Eternal God,
in the fragrance of our praise:
with Jesus Christ our Lord, for evermore.

Alan Gaunt
England

Hungry for ...

Cappuccino
or
expresso, tuna mayo,
chicken tikka,
brown or rye.

All   One hundred per cent pure
fast fresh service,
order welcome,
late or early,
Yet we are still hungry!

Ciabatta
or
foccacia,
almond croissant,
caramel slice,
bun or bap.

All   One hundred per cent pure
fast fresh service,
order welcome,
late or early,
Yet we are still hungry!

Sparkling
or
still water,
hot potato

home-made soup,
nice white sliced.

**All   One hundred per cent pure
         fast fresh service,
         order welcome,
         late or early,
         Yet we are still hungry!**

Christ of feast and picnic,
we treat you like our left-overs.
For all our design foods,
only you can satisfy us.
Change our attitude:
Feed this multitude!

*(To be spoken in a 'rap' style: a different voice could do the 'solo' verses if preferred –
it should sound like the rush of busy office workers grabbing lunch in busy city take-
away cafés.)*

Janet Lees
England

Spring Cleaning

Hey, Jesus,
did you say something about possessions?
Well, it just so happens
that I'd be very pleased
if you'd take some of this stuff
which keeps getting in the way.
For example, that old trunk
filled with ideas which no longer fit.
In the past they've served me well
but now they're tight. They chafe
and are splitting at the seams.
You've given me new garments to grow into.

Over here, I've got stacks of answers
dating back to the days
when life was filled with questions.
You took the questions last collection.
I don't know why I'm hanging on to these.

Down by your feet, are some masks.
I keep accumulating those
in spite of the fact that I promised myself
I'd never wear masks again. They're so heavy!

These bundles are heavy too,
judgmental attitudes wrapped in fear.
Can you help me to move them?

Hey Jesus,
why don't I just hand it all to you
and let you deal with it?
Why don't I just stand here
and admire the results of our spring-cleaning?
You know this house is surprisingly big,
I didn't know I had so much space.
Hey Jesus,
would you like to move in?

Joy Cowley
Aotearoa New Zealand

Every Day

Every day I will offer you,
    loving God, my heart and mind,
every way I discover you
    in the work your hand has signed;
help me see I'm your image, and
    you have dreamed what I might be,
every day in your Spirit,
    I'll find the love and energy!

Every day I will look to Christ,
    and give thanks for wine and bread
through the pain and emptiness
    where your world cries to be fed;
help me see I can work for change,
    and wherever I might be,
every day in your Spirit,
    I'll find the love and energy!

Every day I will take your word,
    answer your compassion's claim,
celebrate every sign of hope,
    every deed done in your name;
help me see you are always there,
    and your light can shine through me,
every day in your Spirit,
    I'll find the love and energy!

Shirley Erena Murray
Aotearoa New Zealand

This Is the Day

Leader   This is the day the Lord has made; we will rejoice and be glad in it.

Response   How can we rejoice?
We have brothers and sisters, all over the country, who must face issues which may affect their rejoicing.

Leader   This is a day of opportunity; a time to remember all those people who face oppression and exploitation of various kinds.

Response   A time to be challenged to greater action and service, to improve the conditions of all who cry out for justice.

Leader	This is not only a day for rejoicing, but a day to seek the truth; a day when we must not turn away into comfortable enclaves of silence.
All	It is a day of hope that the truth will set all people free. Yes, this is the day the Lord has made; we will rejoice and be glad in it.

National Council of Churches
India

Eternal God

Eternal God
We say good morning to you.
Hallowed be your name.
Early in the morning, before we begin our work
we praise your glory.
Renew our bodies as fresh as the morning flowers.
Open our inner eyes, as the sun casts new light upon
    the darkness
which prevailed over the night.
Deliver us from all captivity.
Give us wings of freedom, like the birds in the sky,
to begin a new journey.
Restore justice and freedom as a mighty stream
running continuously as day follows day.
We thank you for the gift of this morning,
and a new day to work with you.

Masao Takenaka
Japan

Help Us To Think and Talk

Lord Jesus:

Help us to think and talk about you enough;
to love you enough and to want you enough,
to bring you to life in our town.

Help us to be aware of you at school,
in the kitchen,
on the floor
phoning our friends
or playing with the cat;
lying in bed making up stories
from the patterns on the ceiling;
when we are making journeys
and when we are still,
when we are noisy
and when we are relaxing,
when we are cross
and when we are laughing,
when we are not thinking of you,
and when we are at prayer.

Brian Louis Pearce
England

Growth

If your life is broken,
do not wrap it up in bandages
but let it lie wide open
to the sun and wind and rain.
Let flowers drop their seeds in.
Plant a tree or two
and encourage the birds
to sing in the branches,
Then invite your friends around
to listen to the music.

If you trust enough to do this,
you will quickly discover
that God has a wonderful way
of turning broken lives
into gardens.

Joy Cowley
Aotearoa New Zealand

Come to the Living Stone

Come to the living stone,
rejected, without worth;
chosen by God to build anew
all things in heaven and earth.

A house that's built on rock
has strength no storm can move;
in Christ we find that we are held
in God's rock-solid love.

As strong foundation stones
carry the building's stress;
Christ takes upon himself the weight
of all our brokenness.

The keystone of the arch
lets stone in air soar free;
so we can risk the dance of life
Christ our security.

The cornerstone supports
each block to make one wall;
together we are bound, the love
of Christ uniting all.

Like living stones we come,
built up in Christ, to be

a vibrant people, healed, renewed
as love's community.

Peter Trow
England

Guided in Silence by a Loving Hand

Alone and in silence I watch the placid lake.
Deceptive water ... now tranquil, now turbulent,
Like life in its make.

Alone and in silence I meet each dawning day.
Confusing hours ... now joyful, now sorrowful,
What do these contrasts say?

O God, alone and in silence let me not be,
Now tranquil, now turbulent, now laughing, now suffering
Alone ... life asks too much of me.

But guided in silence by thy loving hand
In all of life ... now peaceful, now struggling ...
Unafraid I can stand.

Author Unknown
Philippines

Sent Out!

(based on Luke 10:1–9)

A disciple   I'm not sure, Jesus.

Jesus   Not sure about what?

Disciple   Not sure if I'm up to this. I mean, I'm willing to
leave everything behind to be with you, but this
is scary, proclaiming the kingdom and all that.

266

Jesus	You won't be all on your own you know, I'm sending you with others.
Disciple	I know – but you won't be there. And it sounds like you're expecting me to do what you do.
Jesus	Well, yes I am.
Disciple	But I'm not you.
Jesus	You don't have to be. Be yourself. I've shown you the way.
Disciple	But I don't know enough.
Jesus	You know enough.
Disciple	You're throwing me in at the deep end.
Jesus	I suppose I am.
Disciple	I have this list of things I need to do before I will be ready and lots of things I need to take.
Jesus	No. That's not necessary.
Disciple	But in case of emergencies, you know, you can never be too sure.
Jesus	Don't worry. You'll find people who will welcome you. They'll open their homes to you and their hearts to the message. Stay with them.
Disciple	But we may not always get a good reception like that.
Jesus	That's true.
Disciple	We might get thrown out, called names. We might go hungry.
Jesus	That's possible.
Disciple	If that happens what do we do?

Jesus	Move on. There'll be another place that will receive you. Trust me, I think it will be alright.
Disciple	So this kingdom thing – you're sure it has to be this way?
Jesus	I'm afraid so.
Disciple	I hope you know what you're doing. And I hope I don't turn out to be a terrible disappointment to you.
Jesus	I'm sure you won't. You may be surprised by what you can do. You'll have some stories to tell when we get together next!
Disciple	If I survive that is!

Helen Richmond
Australia

Scentered Holiness

Holy God;
from the depths of our hearts,
to the heights of our minds,
you are the enclosing hands,
and the encircling arms.
As we come,
be the one in which we dwell;
be the one in whom we trust –
the path we walk,
the food we eat,
the laughter we enjoy.
Be, to us,
all of life worth living.
And may we see,
touch,
hear,
taste,

and smell your presence
in every moment.
Then the very breath of our joy
may spread your fragrance where we turn.
And,
like early peach blossom,
you may be savoured,
in delighted surprise,
and full cool pleasure,
by the hopeless,
the thirsty
and the lost.

Duncan Tuck
England

And So We Go

(1 Peter 2:4–5)

And so we go, Lord God,
a pilgrim people,
on the path to truth,
called by you,
gathered to you,
that we might be built as living stones for you,
and give to others as from you.

And so we go, Lord God,
to trust you, and to serve others,
for the building of your Kingdom.

In the name of Jesus Christ.

Stephen Brown
England

The God Who Called Abraham

The God who called Abraham to leave his land
  Still calls us to sacrifice.
The God who led his people by the hand
  Still calls us to follow.
The God who walked a royal road to wood and nails
  Still calls us his own.
The God who came like flame-tongues on pilgrims
  Still calls us to life.
  Thanks be to our calling God

Stephen Brown
England

Good News

Good News they say,
good news they want,
  but in the press
  good news is scant.

There's tales of war
and grief and woe;
  and precious few
  the tales that show

A kinder face
and warmer side
  to counteract
  the bad news tide.

And we can feel
too easily
  the world is harsh
  with cruelty

and fail to find
the love that shows
    despite the pain
    compassion grows.

Good news there is
beside the bad
    good news to cheer
    the deeply sad;

good news of life
when all seems gone;
    good news of deeds
    so warmly done;

good news of words
so kindly said;
    good news that winds
    a hopeful thread

within the world
to light the dark
    of hurtful tales
    so cold and stark.

Good news there is
that God is love
    providing all
    we need to have;

good news that God
in Christ has said
    'I am your vine
    I am your bread.'

Good news for all
for life from now
a harvest faith
to tend and grow.

Stephen Brown
England

... A New Song

Great Musician, we sing our praises to you,
the Composer and Conductor of the whole of creation's
symphony
in whom every sphere of earth and heaven rejoices.

Yet we confess that so often our music sounds harsh and discordant ... and that with our broken chords of anger and bitterness we drown your harmonies of joy and compassion.

With the strident blasts of our pride and ambition we overwhelm your serenade of forgiveness and fragment your beautiful melodies of justice and peace.

Forgive us when we only want to play our tune ... when we only choose the good players in our band and leave the rest standing on the street corners of the world, strumming the blues.

Jill Jenkins
England

For Music

Thank you Lord for music
which adds beauty and longing to my life.
You are in the music,
which brings comfort and stillness to my soul
and which sometimes challenges my
complacency.

272

All that is lovely comes from you.
In such may I rest my soul.

William Rutherford
Northern Ireland

We Came Together To Learn

We came together to learn;
we came together to pray;
refugees from Rwanda and Burundi,
pastors from Zaire and Kenya
with a common commitment
to a ministry of reconciliation.
We listened to the stories of conflict and killing;
we shared in the feeling of bleak despair
when it seemed there could be no hope for the future.
Then in the heart of our sharing and praying
we glimpsed the signs of the kingdom
in the courage and faith of men and women
who accept a ministry of reconciliation
even in the face of danger and hostility.
For old rivalries to be forgotten,
for the place of repentance and forgiveness to be found,
for the beginning of the road to justice and reconciliation,
we need to follow in the footsteps
of the crucified and risen Lord,
the Prince of peace.
When women and men of tribes in conflict
agree to talk that way we glimpse the glory of the Kingdom.

John Johansen-Berg
England

In Constant Motion

In constant motion the escalator,
going down to the depths,
rising up to the heights.

A mother, holding her child tightly,
travelling down to the depths, hungry and afraid.
I pass going up to the heights,
satisfied by a recent meal, pocket full of money.
I may not pass this way again; I may miss the moment.
I may reach the heights but doing so
I pass Jesus going down to the depths,
where he will share the hope of resurrection.

John Johansen-Berg
England

A Cry for Help

(Psalm 43)

Stand up for me, God, and help me
    against the loveless mob.
From unjust and slippery rogues
    deliver me unscathed.
In you I have found courage;
    don't now leave me in the lurch.
Why has my life become a misery,
    plagued by mean mockery?

You who are light and truth,
    come and lead me through.
Guide me up to those heights
    where I feel close to you.
Then I'll come to your table,
    to the Lord of celebration.
With music I will praise you,
    God, my true God!

Why have I been so negative,
    why so sour with self-pity?

God is my hope, my saving Lord!
Let the celebrations begin!

Bruce D. Prewer
Australia

The Low Deep Sound

The low deep sound begins in song,
then echoes in the rhythmic movement of the body
and the clapping hands take up the theme,
as we weave together in a symphony of worship.
Voice, feet and hands give praise to God,
as the whole throng, old and young,
women and men, black and white,
express the harmony of a loving searching company.

John Johansen-Berg
England

A Prayer for Preachers

O Lord I pray that the preacher may not be great
If great means that my heart will be drawn to him and not to
you
O Lord I pray that the preacher may not be great
If great means that she will captivate me for an hour but
make no difference to my life.

O Lord I pray that the preacher may not be powerful
If powerful means that I have to pretend I understand
O Lord I pray that the preacher may not be powerful
If powerful makes me feel so incapable of his standards.

O Lord I pray that the preacher may not be persuasive
If persuasive means that I will agree with everything she says
O Lord I pray that the preacher may not be persuasive
If persuasion means obedience to his carefully thought-
through agenda.

O Lord I pray that the preacher is honest
Honest to herself
Honest to his community
Honest to your word
Honest to you.

Edward Cox
England

Grain of Sand

Think not upon yourself as in a moment,
But upon the whole span of your time –
Though miniature your thoughts may be,
As grains within infinity,
Their size belies them not –
For a grain of sand may bend light
Like a jewel ...

And only the perfect bends light,
Which, in its refraction,
Reflects in the infinite moment
The Bloom of the Absolute.

Margot Arthurton
England

Affirmation of Hope

Leader   In the midst of hunger and war
People   We celebrate the promise of plenty and peace.
Leader   In the midst of oppression and tyranny
People   We celebrate the promise of service and
                   freedom.
Leader   In the midst of doubt and despair
People   We celebrate the promise of faith and hope.
Leader   In the midst of fear and betrayal
People   We celebrate the promise of joy and loyalty.
Leader   In the midst of hatred and death

People	We celebrate the promise of love and life.
Leader	In the midst of sin and decay
People	We celebrate the promise of salvation and renewal.
Leader	In the midst of the dying Lord
People	We celebrate the promise of the living Christ.

Edmund Jones
England

A Prayer of Approach and Confession

Holy weaver, loving God
we bow before you in awe, with praise.
In this world of your creating
patterns and threads dance together
in the wonderful web of life.
Threads twining and intertwining,
the world takes shape through your touch.
Seconds pass and a child is born;
minutes tick and more rain drops,
more grains, more flakes are formed;
hours and days and months roll by
and yet more galaxies are seen,
more mountains and valleys explored,
more ideas and possibilities pondered.

Yet as swiftly as you weave,
so we swiftly disentangle.
We uncreate the world through
seeing only for ourselves,
exploring often to destroy or conquer,
pondering sometimes with evil intent.
Forgive us.

Holy mover, living Jesus
we meet before you as companions on the kingdom way.
You came among us,

drawing neighbour to neighbour,
binding enemy to enemy,
teaching us how to weave our lives together
so that we may be more than friends;
showing us how to interlock our concerns with those of
    others
so that together we may bring justice
and tenderness to relationships.

As we move through this world,
often blinkered, many times blind to those around us,
to the needs of the needy, to the wants of the unwanted,
remind us how our paths with others overlap.
When we fail to connect with the cry of our neighbour,
forgive us.
When we fail to feel for the rejected and the lonely,
forgive us.

Holy weaver, life-giving Spirit
we draw near to each other in your presence.
You breathe, and we see afresh;
you startle, and we hear anew;
you cajole, and we act again with vigour.
Weave a pattern of peace between strangers,
weave a pattern of love between friends,
weave a pattern of hope among the hopeless,
weave a pattern of joy among the sorrowful,
weave a pattern of passion between lovers -
for you, holy weaver, creator, son, spirit
are the true lover of us all.
Bind us in your love, now and forever.

Ruth Harvey
England

A Prayer of Thanksgiving and Confession

God of light, life of the world
we bring before you ourselves,
some weary, some tired
from conversation, hard work;
each fragile and vulnerable.

Yet you set before us fresh air
and fresh relationships.
For this we praise you.

God of light
we bring before you our uncertainties,
our confused thoughts,
our worries, our anxieties, our lack of trust.

Yet you set before us
the light of truth and understanding
which knows nothing of right and wrong,
but only knows of love, justice and compassion.
For this we praise you.

God of light
we bring before you our anger,
our despair, our rage, our fury,
our lives hurting with pain and
our minds distraught with fear.

Yet you lay before us
    your open arms – to embrace
    your open ears – to listen
    your open heart – to accept and understand.

For this we praise you.

Ruth Harvey
England

Sometimes When We Pray

Sometimes when we pray we need consciously to close a door on all distractions and concerns, however demanding they may be, then unlatch another door that invites God in, and offer Him room ... and wait there, to welcome Him.

Into the stillness of this place
Into the quiet we are creating
Into the open cavities of our hearts
Come, God of serenity.

Into the twisting mazes of our minds
Into the frailties of our bodies
Into the distractions of our spirits,
Come, God of healing.

From the unspoken fears of our childhood,
From the unresolved tensions of our maturity,
From the apprehensions of our ageing,
Release us, God of freedom.

To those who know and love you,
To those who are on their way to you,
To those who cannot find you
Be present, God of revelation.

Within the encompassing of your power,
Within the enfolding of your peace,
Within the embrace of your possession,
Encircle all your wayward world
Each day and for ever.

Jill Jenkins
England

Gethsemane Prayer

Jesus our brother,
once you knelt sleepless
in the darkness of a garden
alone
and wept and prayed,
sweating, bleeding,
with the pain of powerlessness
with the strain of waiting.
An angel offered you strength –
but it was a bitter cup.

We pray for all
who wake tonight
waiting, agonising,
anxious and afraid,
while others sleep:
for those who sweat
and bleed, and weep alone.

If it is not possible
for their cup to be taken away –
then may they know your presence
kneeling at their side.

Jan Sutch Pickard
England

Leaving

Autumn is orange today
was crimson yesterday
will be yellow tomorrow.

Falling leaves
know the secret of death
glory without sorrow.

Marian Reid
Scotland

Those I Will Meet Today

Thank you Lord
   for the people that I will meet today.
For those who will make my heart ache
   sharing their pain.
Be with them, dear God,
   and give them comfort.
For those who will lift my heart
   sharing their joy.
May they share it also
   with others.
   Remember, dear Lord,
   those who will receive no comfort from others.
Meet them in their need,
   and may they know that they are loved.

William Rutherford
Northern Ireland

Every Person Was Created

Every person was created
by God's glorious grace.
Formed with many variations,
all can find a place;
all have got a special value,
purpose, in the human race.

Young and old from every nation,
one great family
can create, in combination,

282

hope and harmony;
with our different skills and talents,
make one marvellous unity.

With new peace and understanding
all can thrive and grow;
children, adults, learn together
where God's world might go,
if we lean upon each other
what true richness we can know.

We must free our full potential
to respect and care,
God lights up our lives through others,
breaks through everywhere;
lifts his people up triumphant
when we recognise him there.

(Tune: Angel Voices)

Miriam Bennett
England

Called to Become a Perfect Creation

The leader hands round a bowl of stones and asks each person to take one.
As the leader asks people to focus on the stone, gentle music can be played in
the background.

Look at your stone, turn it in your hand.
Think about where it has come from, what secrets it holds.
Once part of the great boulders that shape and form our
   landscape,
part of God's creation: continents and islands, mountains
   and valleys.
Consider its journey – how it has come here,
What forces shaped it, ice and heat and flood, splitting and
pounding, tearing it free, churning and polishing.
Look at it closely.
Is it rough or smooth? Are there sharp edges?

Interesting markings? Lines of colour and beauty? Hidden
    facets?

Now focus on yourself
Where have you come from?
What forces have shaped your journey? Experiences of joy
and of pain, of aloneness and of community?
And what of the person you now are: Are there rough places
or sharp edges? Are there interesting features? Areas of
colour and loveliness?
And what will you become?

You are called to become
A perfect creation.
No one is called to become
Who you are called to be.
It does not matter
How short or tall
Or thick-set or slow
You may be.
It does not matter.

Whether you sparkle with life
Or are silent as a still pool,
Whether you sing your song aloud
Or weep alone in darkness.
It does not matter
Whether you feel loved and admired
Or unloved and alone
For you are called to become
A perfect creation.

No one's shadow
Should cloud your becoming,
No one's light
Should dispel your spark.
For the Lord delights in you,

Jealously looks upon you
And encourages with gentle joy
Every movement of the Spirit
Within you.
Unique and loved you stand,
Beautiful or stunted in your growth
But never without hope and life.
For you are called to become
A perfect creation.
This becoming may be
Gentle or harsh,
Subtle or violent,
But it never ceases,
Never pauses or hesitates,
Only is –
Creative force –
Calling you
Calling you to become
A perfect creation.

Anon.

A Thanksgiving Litany

Leader   We thank you, God.

People   We thank you, God, for who we are.

Leader   Some of us look like the people who lived here long ago, so close to this land that their arrival is not recorded.

People   We thank you, God, for who we are.

Leader   Some of us look like the Spanish, who came in big ships.
    They took the land from the Indians, and thought it was theirs.

People	We thank you, God, for who we are.
Leader	Some of us look like the English, who also came in big ships. They took the land from the Indians and the Spanish, and thought it was theirs.
People	We thank you, God, for who we are.
Leader	Some of us look like the Africans, who also came in big ships. They did not choose to come, and they had no land and no freedom.
People	We thank you, God, for who we are.
Leader	Some of us look like the Asians, who came in big ships across the other ocean. They came looking for work and freedom, and many found discrimination and injustice.
People	We thank you, God, for who we are.
Leader	All of us are different. No two of us look exactly alike. But we are all in the image of God, who came to earth that we might be one.
People	We thank you, God, for who we are, and we pray that you show us what we are to be.

Justo and Catharine González
Cuba

I Can Only Be Me

(This reflection was designed to be passed around a Youth Group, each person reading a line.)

Dear God, you made me, every part of me.
You shaped my body in my mother's womb, and as I have grown over the years.
You live in me, flowing through me like my blood and my breath.

Help me to be all that I am made to be. I can be strong,
    or weak.
I can be rough, or gentle.
I can be funny, happy or upset.
I can do wonderful things, or stuff everything up.
I can only be me, and that's all you ask me to be.
Help me to see myself as you see me.
Then I will know that I am a whole person,
Made especially by you, for your love.

Silvia Purdie
Aotearoa New Zealand

Someday Soon People Will ...

Someday soon people will celebrate life every day.
But we would like to do it right now,
wet and wild and risen with our Lord.
Someday soon people will send up balloons in church.
Turn tired old cathedrals into cafeterias.
Paint gravestones as bright as the sun.
Know that they are beautiful, black, red or white.
Glimpse the face of God in their patient parents.
Use the eyes of friends in place of mirrors.
Bounce through the mountains on beach balls.
Write their Christian names in the sunset.
Become as free as the man called Jesus the Christ.
Sink their teeth into politics for peace.
Turn all bombs into boomerangs.
All bullets into blanks.
Slow down and listen to the Universe.
Slow down and wait for God.
Baptise their babies with love before birth.
Celebrate Easter as angels do below,
And hang Christmas banners on the moon.
Yes someday soon people will live like that,
but we plan to start right now.

Right now Lord. Right now.
Amen, Lord, right now.

Norman Habel
USA

God the Artist

I want to make a rainbow
And paint it with my love,
But first I'll make the paintbox,
Link earth with heaven above.
I'll start off with the dark end
And move towards the light,
Then blend them all together
To make a light that's white.

    We're riding on a rainbow,
    We're riding on a rainbow,
    We're riding on a rainbow,
    That tells us of God's love.

So first I'll make the violet
By touching purple shoots;
The indigo will take longer;
I'll need some deep, dark roots;
The green will not be too hard;
Just wait till spring begins;
For blue I'll need some water
And flashing fishy fins.

The yellow lies on the seashore
And glows in summer sun
The oranges have ripened,
Now autumn has begun.
The red I'll find in winter
In berries on the tree.

Now all my paints are ready,
A miracle you'll see.

For there's another canvas
That isn't in the sky,
A space in every person,
A heart where tears can cry,
A place where joy can spring up
Like sunshine after rain,
A gentle creamy paper
Where I can paint again.

I'll use those same old colours
With which I paint the sky,
Remind them of the promise
I made in years gone by,
Recall in them my loving,
My caring for my world,
Each time they see the rainbow
Across the earth unfurled.

Text and tune: Marian

June Boyce-Tillman
England

Networking

The hope goes round,
And the strength goes round,
And the power goes round,
And the love goes round;
And hands are joined
And our hearts are joined,
And the Spirit is flowing between us.

Wind circles that will encircle
The earth, the sky and the deep abyss;

Find loving entwined in networking,
Claiming the strength that's our birthright.

For God, our God
Is a hoping God,
And a strength'ning God,
An empowering God;
And God, our God
Is a woven God,
And the warp and the weft of creation.

Dance joy in a cosmic circle
A toughness strand in the cloth of God;
Weave shapes of a true integrity;
This is the stuff of creation.

Tune: Greensleeves (as arranged by June Boyce-Tillman)

June Boyce-Tillman
England

Commitment to Creation

We shall go out renewed in our commitment
To integrate creation in ourselves,
To work and trust,
To hope and play and wonder
With hearts that long for world integrity.
We'll work to right the wrongs of devastation
Of humankind and all created life;
We'll dream our dreams of earth's reintegration
Within the dreamtime of a Christ who is the Way.

We'll play our games that still the hectic struggle
To win a race that all can only lose;
We'll trust the God who works from deep within us
For peace and justice, unity for all.
We'll keep alive the flame of hope within us
And wonder still at beauty yet unborn.

We'll leap and dance the resurrection story,
Including all within the circles of our love.
(Tune: Londonderry)

June Boyce-Tillman
England

The Woman at the Well

An exhibit in Liverpool Anglican Cathedral, UK, focused on the woman at the well who is regarded by the Eastern Orthodox Churches as a saint. She was canonised and named St Photina, the bringer of light.

She is the first of Christ's followers to be recorded as having gone out and spread the good news of the Gospel. We do not know her name or what became of her but we do know that she was real.

Her figure dominated the display. She was faceless and unknown, the 'mother' of all those women who have preached the Gospel over the centuries. She was dressed in clothes easily recognised as those of a preacher.

From her hands blue ribbons flowed to represent the water of life given to her by Christ. The 'water' flowed outwards both to her successors and to the well. On the ribbons and in the well were cards, in the colours of water, on which local women had written their thoughts, feelings and hopes for their church.

Walking out from the well were the figures of women. They were intended to be nearly invisible, sidelined, downtrodden, and constructed from the elements of mother earth. There were women in outline only. These represented the invisible christian women of history who remain unnamed and forgotten. There was a mother figure which represented the pivotal role of women as mothers. One figure was made from water and one from grain and seeds, the means of sustaining life. In most of the world it is women who fetch water, gather food and tend the soil.

A figure covered in dead leaves represented all the women who have lived and died for Christ. A figure covered in living plants represented the women of today still carrying the light of Christ out into their world.

Together, the figures symbolised an unbroken link to the first preacher.

Kay Andrews
England

We Are the Church

Loving God, we strive to be your church in our world but we need to recognise that there is a diversity in our midst. We have different ways to express our love for you in our worship. As your people we have different needs and expectations. Our hopes and our dreams, our backgrounds and our visions are not always the same. Grant that we may find and create ways to work together in community. Help us to hear each other in love. Help us to be open to the needs of others. Give us the will to find ways to be the church in our communities. The world needs the message of love and hope that we carry. Help us to find excitement in our individuality, harmony in our discord and unity in our diversity. Grant that all we do, we do out of love for you and for humankind.

Betty Radford Turcott
Canada

Mother Teresa and the Beggar Boy

One day Mother Teresa came back from her work in the slums. As she walked to her residence, a beggar boy stood suddenly in front of her and asked her to accept his income of

292

that day: ten rupees. Mother Teresa was very surprised and at first she refused, saying to the boy, 'Oh no, you have earned this little money for yourself, for your own food.' But the boy insisted that she accept the money. Reluctantly she took the ten rupees. She said that the boy was happier than she had ever seen anyone who had given her a lot of money.

Involuntarily we are reminded of the bible story of the widow and her two small coins,* of whom Jesus says, 'Truly, I tell you, this poor widow has put in more than all those who are contributing to the treasury. For all of them have contributed out of their abundance; but she out of her poverty has put in everything she had, all she had to live on.'

This is a true story, that I heard from Mother Teresa, when I was a theological student at Bishop's College in Calcutta.

* Mark 12:41–4

Paul Sarker
Bangladesh

For Our Land

Thank you Lord for this beautiful land of ours; for its fertile fields and wide rivers, the boats sailing, the fishermen catching the tasty fish, its golden fields of rice and jute, the juicy sugar canes and the palms. Fruits are many in their season; mangoes, bananas and jack fruits, beautiful flowers full of colours and fragrance and the song of the cuckoo and melody of the Doel. Thank you Lord for its people, language and culture, its poets and writers and bards and great sons and daughters. Thank you Lord for our families that hold us together in joy and loving care. Lord give us thankful hearts that we may make this country a place where we may live in harmony and in justice and the poor will not be forgotten. Bless our leaders that they may work for the good of their country and build a harmonious relationship with our neighbours.

Bishop B. D. Mondal
Bangladesh

Malagasy Hospitality

In Madagascar, when you feel lost in an unknown situation, the safest place to go is the church. There is always someone to receive you. This is partly a manifestation of Malagasy hospitality. Also, this is the real manifestation of a caring Church, the living image of God. God through His Church, always welcomes strangers no matter who they are or where they come from. There is always room for anybody who knocks at the door. The living condition of the Church is its deeds towards needy people. We should know by now that actions are more important than words. There are many uprooted people around the world who seek refuge and shelter, with a load of despair and bitterness but full of hope. They feel lost and knock at the door of the church! Welcome them as God welcomes you!

Ranto Ranaivoson
Madagascar

Creator God

(Short writings which can be used in various situations)

Creator God, I saw the earth from space,
    so beautiful.
I saw the water, land and air
    for all the people.
Let every person care for every place.
Let those with plenty share with those without.
Let every life have love and gladness.

O God, we know your love in the baby
in the manger.
Let us know your love in the child
deprived.
O God, as people came to the stable
with gifts and wonder
Let us go to those less strong and able,
with care and comfort.

O God, I see your face smiling, thinking, crying
with Mary and Martha.
Let me see your face in the people I meet in the street,
at work, at home today:
the smiles, the hidden thoughts and tears.

O God, the rain's been pouring down for hours.
The day's depressing, dull and dreary,
yet I hear – the birds are singing to your glory!
When my heart is heavy
let my spirit rise to sing a song
in celebration, even so.

As, O God, I take my morning shower,
let your love refresh my spirit,
let your presence warm my heart,
let me be your blessing to my neighbours through the day.

As, O God, I take my evening shower,
let your love wash from my shoulders
hurts and heaviness,
let your cleansing presence bring me peace,
let me rest contented in your care throughout this night.

O God, as I make my way, preoccupied, head down,
let me lift my eyes to see the flowers, the trees, the hills,

let me lift my eyes to see the faces of the people,
– and know your loving presence all around me.

Leader   O God, let us know your love close to us.

Everyone   Creator, let us know your love around us.
Spirit, let us know your fire within us,
Saviour, let us know your peace enfolding us.

Leader   O God, let each one, woman, man, youth, child,
know your love.

Everyone   Creator, let each one know their preciousness.
Spirit, let each one be standing tall and strong.
Saviour, let each one have someone with your
love.

Leader   O God, let us rest, knowing your love for us.

Everyone   Creator, let us sleep in the assurance
of a new day tomorrow.
Spirit, let us sleep in the confidence
of your care through the night.
Saviour, let us sleep knowing
we have done our best,
and that is enough.

John Hunt
Aotearoa New Zealand

Peace

Peace can only be manifested in society when there is peace
within the human heart. The cause of peace is sometimes
pursued with aggressiveness. This is the case when peace is no
more than a concept or an ideal.

Peace communicates itself wordlessly. In India the great example of the power of peace was seen in Mahatma Gandhi whose inner peace influenced the whole nation.

Work for peace must first of all be a work within ourselves.

Bede Griffiths
India

Beyond Alice Springs

God of wandering camels
    and faraway places,
of remote red gorges
    and Aboriginal faces;

God of deep silences
    and awesome setting sun,
of the moonlit plains
    and dingoes on the run;

God of broken droughts
    and creek beds flowing,
of inland daisy fields
    and the desert pea growing;

God of immense horizons
    and of blowing sand;
confront us and teach us
    within this cryptic land.

Bruce D. Prewer
Australia

Day's End

At end
of day my bruises set the mood;
the toil

seems rarely worth the scant reward.
I turn
to prayer, wondering if all is vain,
if dust
is dust and ever shall remain.
But then
I ride the dolphins of Christ's dreams
and know
that life is higher than it seems.

Bruce D. Prewer
Australia

Caring for the Church

(as it struggles to know the will of God in issues of sexuality)

This is costly
because it deeply divides the church
in an agony of soul.
There are those who cannot understand
why it is an issue at all and who believe
that the Bible speaks plainly on the matters at stake.
And there are those who,
with just as much conviction, believe
the Bible bears witness to another possibility.

Meanwhile homosexual people, who are
always the loved children of God, and
the rest of the church, wait and suffer
together in the search for truth.

Take Away the Dark Glass

Take away the dark glass
which stands between our human wisdom
and your truth, O God of grace.
The waiting to see clearly,
and the pathway towards

understanding how to love in your name,
is too long, loving Christ,

We wound each other deeply on the way.
We bleed in the agony of our choices
and the terrible separations
which open like unbridgeable chasms before us.

All this in your name, O God.
All this is the struggle to be true.
Come close to us, Holy Spirit.
Stand in your light before us
on the way.

Uniting Church in Australia
National Commission for Mission

The Face of Love

I had to work out if our love was exclusive or not. Did the love of God rule out the other loves of my life? Was he in fact jealous? With some people it does not seem that the relationship is like that.

I increasingly came to see him not as a rival to other loves but as part of them. I looked into someone else's face with love, and found him present. He in fact showed me what love looks like – its true face.

Lionel Blue
England

Dreaming in a New Reality

Nyungar*   Creator Maman*, you spoke to us through the Dreamtime.

Wadjella*   Creator God, enrich us with some under-standing of Aboriginal spirituality.

Nyungar	Creator Maman, your spirit moved across Australia linking all Aboriginal people through the tracks and songlines of our land.
Wadjella	Creator God, help us to continue to dispel the myth of Terra Nullius.
Nyungar	Creator Maman, you gave us our heritage through our dance, song and sacred sites. We find ourselves still struggling in this society today, against another law which fails to fully recognise our identity or heritage.
Wadjella	Creator God, help us to continue to stand alongside our sisters and brothers in their struggle for justice, equality and self-determination.
All	Reconciling God, Maman, Creator of the wind, land and all living things, bring us together so that together we can build friendships, trust and love.

Nyungar is an Aboriginal person in South West Australia
Wadjella is a white person
Maman is Nyungar for God

Uniting Church in Australia
National Commission for Mission

Spiral of Life

My heart speaks of former beliefs,
Embraced by a God of nature,
Centred on the sacred earth.
The green spiral of life begs for my return.
The small circle I was concerned with was so safe,
I chose only that which I wanted to see.
Now my vision has broadened,

The white of *naivete* has become a blinding light,
Exposing me to the reds of anger and purple,
Woman's unfair share.
Purple life spirals,
Searching for ways to remove stones,
Looking for rainbows, symbols of hope.
And then there is space,
Spirit space, where the breath of God transforms,
Allowing diversive thinking.
Space to move in;
Space to change in;
Space to grow in;
There must always be space!

JoAnn Symonds
Canada

Woman's Creed

I believe in God, the origin of heaven and earth,
        the beginning of all creation.
    The Lord has created man and woman
          in the Lord's own image, filled them with Spirit
          and let them govern the earth together.

I believe in God's creation. How wonderful is the body
        You have made!
    I believe that body is what You are pleased with; it is
    of holiness;
        it is what You have bestowed upon us,
          which is not to be assaulted with violence.
    Woman's body, though abused, trampled, violated,
        I would not have it despised;
    My own body, should it be violently assaulted,
    sexually
        assaulted, raped; I would never feel ashamed of.
    In God's mercy, I lift up my head and
        rebuke those who assaulted woman's body.

I believe in God, who has assured woman's dignity;
My feet will no longer be bound by feudal practice:
My menses has shaken off the ignorant accusation of
'the unclean';
My breasts, waist, legs, skin and looks are
integral parts of my whole, where indecent
peeps
and molestation are not allowed;
The 'beauty' I own is no longer the merchandise in
shop windows and TV commercials,
or objects of the rogue's sexual desires,
Nor my 'ugliness' the excuse of those who wish to
bring me down.

I believe in God whose love gives me life.
My body is God's continued creation.
Foetus in my womb proclaims the wonders of
procreation.
I firmly believe in life's dignity: for all lives come from
God.
Both man and woman have the right to live.
Female babies, no longer be killed as a result of clan's
discrimination of their inheritance rights:
Male babies, no longer be born for the sheer sake of
family
wealth and traditions.
I deeply believe, this is a beautiful world,
a world under God's care.
I am willing, most willing, to help reveal again
the beauty of his world.

Alison Lee
Hong Kong

Credo

I believe in God
who did not create an immutable world

302

a thing incapable of change
who does not govern according to eternal laws
that remain
inviolate
or according to a natural order
of rich and poor
of the expert and the ignorant
of rulers and subjects

I believe in God
who willed conflicts in life
and wanted us to change the status quo
through our work
through our politics

I believe in Jesus Christ
who was right when he
like each of us
just another individual who couldn't beat city hall
worked to change the status quo
and was destroyed
looking at him I see
how our intelligence is crippled
our imagination stifled
our efforts wasted
because we do not live as he did

every day I am afraid
that he died in vain
because he is buried in our churches
because we have betrayed his revolution
in our obedience to authority
and our fear of it
I believe in Jesus Christ
who rises again and again in our lives
so that we will be free
from prejudice and arrogance

from fear and hate
and carry on his revolution
and make way for his kingdom

I believe in the Spirit
that Jesus brought into the world
in the brotherhood of all nations
I believe it is up to us
what our earth becomes
a vale of tears starvation and tyranny
or a city of God

I believe in a just peace
that can be achieved
in the possibility of a meaningful life
for all people
I believe this world of God's
has a future
amen

Dorothee Sölle
Germany

World-wide

Beckoning Christ,
you call us out of our comfortable ghettos of 'us' and 'them'
to risk discipleship without walls.

You call us into a world-wide fellowship
where God is worshipped
above all other.

You call us into a world-wide fellowship
where prayer is offered
day and night.

You call us into a world-wide fellowship
where we can share what we are
with others who love you.

You call us into a world-wide fellowship
where each person has something to give
to the whole.

You call us into a world-wide fellowship
where compassion and respect
shape missionary endeavour.

Keep on beckoning us
out of our safe havens
into your richer fellowship
of challenge and reconciliation, faith and hope.

Kate Compston
England

Evangelism

Evangelism is only made real
in the context of the life
of the people and must speak
to their needs.

Evangelism among Aboriginal
people is linked with the
development of Aboriginal
theology.

Evangelism must reach into
every area – economic,
social, political.

Evangelism must involve
the rebuilding of people's
lives and community.

Evangelism must be
immediately related to
social issues and linked
with a fight to right
wrong.

Besides proclamation,
worship, fellowship and
service perform an
evangelical function.

Evangelism through word
of mouth cannot be
separated from the things
we do with our hands.

Uniting Aboriginal and Islander
Christian Congress
Australia

Come, Great Spirit

Spirit of celestial fire,
enlighten us — lift our spirits
   where your light silvers sapphire air
   and angels sing do-not-be-afraid;
   where our vision arches
   past the bend in the road
   and over the rainbow;
   where we can see
   the forest for the trees,
   the stars beyond our equations,
   and the wings of the morning
   beating back the night.

Spirit of freshening wind,
move us — change our point of view
 **until we can see our neighbour's pain
 as our own;**
 until we can view our enemy
 as estranged family;
 **until we can lift other spirits
 as you have lifted ours.**

Spirit of descending love,
bring us back to earth —
 our eyes glowing silver-sapphire,
 our hearts warm with angel song.
**Spirit of fire, wind and love,
abide with us and make us
kindred spirits.**

Norm S. D. Esdon
Canada

Now!

Lord, at this moment I sort
 of feel good towards you
 as if you do make sense
 after all – know what I mean?
Help me to cherish this 'now'.
 Sometimes, no not only sometimes
 often times I think it's
 all a sham, a fantasy
 when I look at my life
 and the lives of others.
But then Lord, you keep coming
 through, somehow – I see a
 flower, a child, a smile,
 a painting – I hear a
 bird, a song, a laugh
 a brook – I feel the

rain, the sun, the wind
the snow.
And then Lord, you do make sense
after all – like now
as I sit quietly – I give you
some space, let you breathe
with me – it is good.
Thank you Lord, for this moment
for this Now –
Help me to cherish.

Carys Humphreys
Wales/Taiwan

God Our Reconciler

God our Reconciler,
Who, in the person of the Spirit, beckons us into community,
guides us into the paths of peace
and inspires our longing to become more Christ-like;
let your hand nudge us into the adventure
of painting new visions, writing new words,
building new structures, and carving new landmarks
to meet the challenges of our time.
As you embrace us, may our hands embrace the world
to find that all our sisters and brothers – all living things –
share the same pulse of God-given life.

Kate Compston
England

Called To Be Church

'... the Church is meant to be: a laboratory of peace, a
parable of the Kingdom, a sign of contradicton among the
nations, a place of welcome amidst the sectarianism and
xenophobia of the surrounding society, a community of
praise ...'

(Brother Leonard of Taizé)

308

Our God, you call us to be Church: enable us to create – across cultural, age and class boundaries – a laboratory of peace, testing out your vision of community and love as we struggle to live with our differences.

Our God, you call us to be Church: enable us to be a parable of the Kingdom, allowing the upside-down values of your commonwealth to nudge us away from the acquisitive and self-regarding attitudes of our day.

Our God, you call us to be Church: enable us to be a sign of contradiction among the nations, pointing to hope in the midst of disillusion, offering non-violent resistance when evil threatens, accepting loss of prestige or wealth in the cause of justice.

Our God, you call us to be Church: enable us to be a place of welcome and warmth, where what is ignored elsewhere may be heard and honoured, where sorrows may be shared and our stories told, where hard questions may be asked and new ideas greeted with joy.

Our God, you call us to be Church: enable us to be a community of praise, cracking open the dry husks of cynicism and despair, being clowns and jesters for Christ, celebrating the mystery of faith in stillness and song.

Kate Compston
England

God of All Living

God of all living,
we have seen your presence
in the rhythm and surprises of our years.
You have accompanied us through all that is past.
So we thank you.

We recognise your closeness
in this day.
You challenge and encourage us in each act and decision.
So we praise you.

Now we look for you
in the promises which stretch before us.
You meet us with hope
and call us to freedom
to live as your new people.
So we trust you
and commit ourselves again,
to live as risen Christians.

Michael Durber
England

Come Holy Spirit

Come Holy Spirit, set your Church on fire
    Strike it as the lightning hits a reaching spire
        Burn away the structures and consume the sham
            Of our holy systems, come in Jesus' name.

Blow away the cobwebs of our stubborn past
    Come blow up among us, myths unfit to last
        Wind of change, pursue us and disturb our calm
            Teach us what true love is, take our hearts
            by storm.

Come Holy Spirit, convict, convert and consecrate us. If the
doors of our hearts are closed to the coming in of your Spirit,
then break them open, come in and never leave us again.

Evangeline Rajkumar
India

Spirit of God

Spirit of God pervading the earth as swirling mist,
enveloping creation, her presence shall persist;
she rests on men and women, she shares her gifts with all,
and we respond in freedom, rejoicing at her call.

Her wisdom keeps creating new wonders to behold,
through her creation's story is constantly retold.
Mountain and river valley acclaim her name with praise,
the glacier and the desert as one their voices raise.

Midst folk she freely mingles to challenge and inspire,
dream dreams and share visions, rekindle sparks of fire,
a passion for God's mission we all are called to share
'til heaven and earth both mirror *koinonia* and care.

Spirit of God empowering each of us as we sing,
our faith-skills and whole being before you now we bring.
Embrace us with your blessing, transform us through your
    Word,
so we may live confessing the love and grace of God.
(Tune: Passion Chorale)

Lindsey Sanderson
Scotland

Messenger of Marvels

Messenger of marvels, challenger of sleep,
Light is born – and quickens life within the deep.
God, quicken us, empower and set us free:
Light is come, like treasure salvaged from the sea.

Truths, obscured and buried, speak in language plain;
Old wells are unstopped, and water springs again.
Once locked in folly, now we find the key:
Truth is come, like treasure salvaged from the sea.

311

Beauty's gold is rescued, dross is skimmed away;
Hoards from secret places shine anew today.
Give we our hearts to God's fierce alchemy:
Beauty comes, like treasure salvaged from the sea.

Love of Christ, rejected, buried in the tomb,
Now is resurrected, leaps the prison-room.
Called out* from death, Christ's living Body, we:
Love is come, like treasure salvaged from the
sea.

Secret, silent Kingdom – jettisoned, denied –
Rises from the deep and dances on the tide:
In and around us, waiting patiently:
Kingdom come! like treasure salvaged from the sea.

*Ekklesia *(Church) is that which is 'called out'* ...
(Tune: Noel Nouvelet)

Kate Compston
England

Weaving

Poets weave words that teach our tongues the facets of our
faith.

Poets weave words that send our souls soft singing on their
way.

Poets weave words that linger long and murmur in our
minds.

Poets weave words that wander wilfully within our worship.

Poets weave words that rhyming we remember.

312

Poets weave words.

They cannot do otherwise.

Marjorie Dobson
England

Visual Prayer Ideas

To give thanks:

Place a drawing of a vase with stems coming from it on a large piece of paper at the front of the church. As people enter they should be given a simple flower shape cut from brightly coloured paper and a leaf shape from green paper. At the appropriate time in the service for prayers of thanksgiving, they are asked to write on the flower something for which they wish to give thanks. These are then collected by children, if this is in the context of All Age Worship, or placed in the offertory plates and stuck on the stems in the picture as the prayers are prayed by the worship leader. Later, in worship, the leaves are used in a similar manner for the prayers of intercession, the leader drawing these prayers together, while sticking them onto the stems.

For the healing of the nations:

A drawing of a bare tree on a large piece of paper should be placed at the front of the church. Items for intercessory prayer are written on paper leaf shapes and then collected. Following the reading of Revelation 22.1–6, the leaf shapes are stuck on the tree while being read out to form the prayers.

Making something beautiful for God:

This is most easily used when there are two occasions for worship on the same day using a theme such as Vocations Sunday or Unemployment Sunday. Small hand shapes are given to each person as they enter the church, and then at an appropriate point in worship they are collected. People could

313

write their names on them first as a sign of offering themselves and their hands for God's work. Between the worship times these are stuck onto a large piece of paper, fanned out and overlapped to produce the tail of a bird – the head and body shape having been stuck on. This can then be used to emphasise the point that when we all work together and each part of the body does its work we can produce something beautiful for God.

Jenny Spouge
England

One Life

He was born in a stable,
in an obscure village,
From there he travelled,
Less than 200 miles.

He never won an election,
He never went to college,
He never owned a home,
He never had a lot of money.

He became a nomadic preacher,
Popular opinion turned against him,
He was betrayed by a close friend,
And his other friends turned away.

He was unjustly condemned to death,
Crucified on a cross among common thieves,
On a hill overlooking the town dump,
And when dead, laid in a borrowed grave.

Nineteen centuries have come and gone,
Empires have risen and fallen,

Mighty armies have marched,
And powerful rulers have reigned.

Yet no one has affected men as much as he,
He is the central figure of the human race,
He is the Messiah, the Son of God,
Jesus Christ.

'He is the image of the unseen God,
And the first-born of all creation,
For in him were created all things,
in heaven and on earth' (Colossians 1:15–16).

Kristone
East Asia

Easter Reflections

He is not here, for he is risen (Matthew 28:6).

Easter brings a message of hope. Out of an empty tomb, the risen Christ fills the earth with love and hope. Death is not the end. Decay is not the order of the day. Despair is temporary. Hope is life and while there is life, there is hope.

Easter is a time of joy. In the midst of Mary's mourning and anxiety, the risen Christ calls her by name, 'Mary'. And she replied, 'Rabboni'. Easter is a time of joy because it is a special time of recognising, communing, and rejoicing. Easter is a time of blessing because it is a time of sacred naming.

Do you recognise the face of Christ in each other?
Do you commune and relate with each other in such a way that people really wonder how do you do it? Do you rejoice at the simple miracles of everyday life? If you do, then Easter matters to you.

Easter is community time. It is a time to reach out to others.
The risen Christ reached out to the women who went to the tomb.
The risen Christ reached out to the men who betrayed him.
The risen Christ had breakfast with the disciples at the beach.
The risen Christ tells Simon Peter to feed his lambs.
The risen Christ calls us to reach out to others.

We are not meant to be alone. We are not meant to wallow in grief and despair. We are not meant to eat by ourselves. But rather, we are meant to commune, to share rice or eat fish or break bread together equally. Easter time is community time. Let us live Easter time all the time!

Elizabeth Tapia
Philippines

For Communion

Invitation

Come now to God's feast:
come from east and west and north and south.
Come with the widow who had only two mites,
come with the poor who are always with us,
come with the children who the disciples tried to turn away,
come with the woman who touched his cloak,
come with all who followed him.
Come with your needs, your doubts, your questions.
Most of all, come as you are;
with the confidence you have and the confidence you lack.
Come now and keep the feast.

Blessing

Blessed bread,
how the poor yearn for you;
how the rich squander you.

From the Breadmaker,
to the bread taker:
Blessed, heavenly bread.

Concluding prayer

Companion Christ, True Vine,
we have eaten heavenly bread.
We have drunk the wine of promise.
We commit ourselves to a life of kinship.
Sustain us on the road
that in partnership with the poor,
we may travel on to eat and drink
in justice and peace
in the vineyard of the Vinegrower.

Janet Lees
England

Your Body

(at the sharing of bread and wine)

Voice 1   This is my body,
broken by abuse;
cigarette burns on my skin,
stack of reports for the public enquiry.

All   **This is your body.**

Voice 2   This is my body,
distended by malnutrition;
flies around my eyes,
a small figure in world economics.

All   **This is your body.**

Voice 3   This is my body,
imprisoned by attitudes
that see only stick or chair;
object of derision and exclusion.

317

All	**This is your body.**

Leader	Disabled Christ,
	    broken by torture,
	    abuse and the struggle for power,
	live in us;
	that what burns today may be issues,
	where even the smallest figures count,
	that none are derided or excluded
	from your feast of life.

	As we break this bread we celebrate your broken body, hanging on a cross, struggling in the church, liberated in the world.
All	**We are the body of Christ, We are many yet we are one body, sharing one bread.**

Janet Lees
England

Breaking the Crown

Born to be King
Jesus took the crown
and broke it
so that we may know life.

Born to be King
Jesus took people
and moulded them
so that we may know God.

Born to be King
Jesus took the things of life

and wove stories
so that we may know the Kingdom.

He took Kingship
and broke it
into servanthood.
Moulded it
into sorrow
and wove
a new path to follow.

We take bread,
broken
into remembrance.
We take wine
poured out.

We follow a woven path
broken, remoulded.
Citizens of a Kingdom
turned upside down.
Subjects of a monarchy
committed to service.
Tellers of stories
fit to proclaim a King.
We who are the Salt and the Light
enter through the narrow gate
that is the way of God.

Craig Muir
England

With Open Hands of Welcome, Lord

With open hands of welcome, Lord,
accepting all that love entails;
risking rejection, hurt, despair;
open to feel the bite of nails;

you invite to the table, all
who come in weakness, need and loss,
and you redeem our lives with hope
born of the suffering of your cross.

Jesus, to share the Kingdom's feast,
in joy your people gather here.
You heal the Body's brokenness,
breaking the chain of guilt and fear.
Only the story of your grace
which now the bread and wine relate,
can shape the open hands of love
out of the fists of human hate.

We celebrate an opened grave,
rejoice in love that will not die,
proclaim anew the Easter faith,
death swallowed up in victory.
Here, as you meet us, Risen Christ,
new life begins and love breaks free;
heaven and earth at last are one,
promise becomes reality.

Our thanks to you, Lord Jesus Christ;
you shared our human joy and pain,
suffered the cross and broke the tomb
so that God's love and peace might reign.
We give our lives to you in praise:
may every word and act express
how beautiful it is to know
in you God's total faithfulness.

Peter Trow
England

An African Farewell

Leader   *Bagaetsho* go in peace and may the rain go with you.

Congregation Amen.

Leader   May the God of our ancestors; the God of Kgama, Sechele and Bathoeng* keep you safe.

Congregation Amen.

Leader   May the God of love journey with you
May the God of creation keep you
May the God of history dwell in your homes

Congregation Amen.

* These are the three chiefs that embraced the Christian faith for themselves and their subjects. They fought for the liberation of Botswana from the Boers of South Africa and sought protection from the British Crown. They are our Heroes.

Prince Dibeela
Botswana

A Blessing

The creative power of God go with us.
The compassionate love of Jesus go with us.
The driving force of the Spirit go with us,
As we follow our calling to link God to his people.

Marjorie Dobson
England

Index

Acknowledgements

The compiler and publisher acknowledge with thanks permission to reproduce copyright.

* *Text can be copied for use in worship on a one-off, non-commercial basis using this acknowledgement.*

** *Used by permission.*

'A Blessing', © Marjorie Dobson from *Open with God*, published by the West Yorkshire Synod of the Methodist Church.

'A Cry for Help', © Bruce D. Prewer from *More Australian Psalms*, Openbook Publishers, 205 Halifax Street, Adelaide, South Australia 5000.

'A Friend Is One Who Comes To You', © Helen Worth.

'A Great Country', © Revd Dr C. M. Kao.

'A Litany for Urban Ministry', © John Campbell, South Aston United Reformed Church, Birmingham B6 5ET UK.

'A Litany of Tears', © Richard Becher.

'A Litany on Community Sharing', © Elizabeth S. Tapia.

'A Mother's Prayer', © Bob Commin, c/o Mercer Books, 5 Roslyn Road, Rondebosch, Cape Town, South Africa.

'... A New Song', © Jill Jenkins, 61 Lakeside Road, London N13 4PS UK.

'A Patchwork Prayer', © Revd Jean Mortimer, 15 L'Espec Street, Northallerton, North Yorkshire, DL7 8QY UK.

'A People's Lamentation On Human Rights Day' Sharon Rose Joy Ruiz-Duremdes. **

'A Plea', © Kate Compston from *Word in the World*, published by the National Christian Education Council (NCEC). **

'A Prayer for a Party', © Ruth Harvey. Director of the Ecumenical Spirituality Project of the Council of Churches for Britain and Ireland.

'A Prayer for Detained Asylum Seekers', from *Keeping Hope Alive*, published by the Jesuit Refugee Service, 162 Stockwell Road, London SW9 9TQ.**

'A Prayer for Preachers', © Edward Cox.

'A Prayer of Approach and Confession', © Ruth Harvey, Director of the Ecumenical Spirituality Project of the Council of Churches for Britain and Ireland.

'A Prayer of Longing and Letting Go', © Kate Compston. First appeared in *Connect*, a publication of The Methodist Church.

'A Prayer of Thanksgiving and Confession', © Ruth Harvey, Director of the Ecumenical Spirituality Project of the Council of Churches for Britain and Ireland.

'A Song for Peace', © Aaron Kramer.

'A Sower's Farewell', © Amado L. Picardal.

'A Teardrop Falls', © Craig Neil Muir.*

'A Thanksgiving Litany', inspired by essays of Puerto Rican school children in New York City, in I*n Accord – Let Us Worship* by Justo and Catherine González. Copyright © 1981 by Friendship Press, Inc.**

'A Time to Keep Silence', © David Jenkins from *Further Everyday Prayers*, published by the National Christian Education Council (NCEC).**

'A Touching Place', from *Love From Below* (Wild Goose Publications, 1989), John L. Bell and Graham Maule, copyright © 1989 WGRG, Iona Community, 840 Govan Road, Glasgow G51 3UU, Scotland.

'A World of Difference – Again', from *The Song of The Sparrow*, published by The Leprosy Mission England and Wales, 1991.

'Aboriginal Justice', © Anne Pattel-Gray.

'Adnabod', from *Dail Pren*, Waldo Williams; publishers Gomer Press. Translation by Noel Davies.**

338

'Advent Feet', ** The Presbyterian Church of Aotearoa New Zealand.

'Affirmation of Hope', Edmund Jones from *Worship and Wonder*, Stainer and Bell.**

'All in a Day's Work', © Valerie Shedden

'All It Needs', © Richard Becher.

'An Advent Call to Worship', © Edward Cox.

'An African Farewell', © Prince Dibeela.

'And So We Go', © Stephen Brown. * and **

'And the Bread and the Fish Continue To Multiply ...', Glenn Jetta Barclay.**

'Anzac Dawn', E. Body, Presbyterian Church of Aotearoa New Zealand.**

'Apoi', © Amil Netto.

'At Home in the City', © John Campbell, South Aston United Reformed Church, Birmingham B6 5ET UK.*

'Awareness of God Everywhere', © William Rutherford. Written during a Retreat on Celtic Spirituality, Corrymeela, Northern Ireland.

'Be Still and Know', © Carys Humphreys.

'Be Still and Know That I Am God', ** The Presbyterian Church of Aotearoa New Zealand.

'Be Strong and Courageous', © Helen Worth.

'Because You Came', Shirley Erena Murray, © Hope Publishing Co/CopyCare, PO Box 77, Hailsham BN27 3EF UK.

'Beyond Alice Springs', © Bruce D. Prewer from *More Australian Psalms*, Openbook Publishers, 205 Halifax Street, Adelaide, South Australia 5000.

'Birth Pangs', Ruben Alves. Permission sought.

'Blossom', © Valerie Shedden.

'Break the Chain', © Stephen Brown. * and **

'Breaking the Crown', © Craig Neil Muir.*

'Bridge of Peace', © Kate Compston from *Word in the World*, published by the National Christian Education Council (NCEC).**

'Bringing Harmony', copyright © Christopher Herbert from *Prayers for Children* (National Society/Church House Publishing, 1993). Reproduced by permission.

'Brother, Sister I'm Beside You', ** The Presbyterian Church in Aotearoa New Zealand.

'Brought to Life', © Kate Compston.

'Burned Church', © Margot Arthurton.

'By the Lake of Galilee', © Maureen Edwards.

'Café', © Brian Louis Pearce. From *Jack o' Lent; Headpieces* (Stride, 1991).*

'Called to Account', © Feiloaiga Taule'ale'ausumai.

'Called To Be Church', © Kate Compston from *Word in the World* published by the National Christian Education Council (NCEC). **

'Called to Become a Perfect Creation', anon.

'Caring for the Church', © Uniting Church in Australia, National Commission for Mission.

'Carol of the Epiphany' (I sought him dressed in finest clothes), from *Innkeepers and Light Sleepers* (Wild Goose Publications, 1992), words and music by John L. Bell, copyright © 1992 WGRG, Iona Community, 840 Govan Road, Glasgow G51 3UU, Scotland.

'Celebrate All Human Beauty', Shirley Erena Murray, © Hope Publishing Co/CopyCare.

'Celebration', © Joy Cowley. Published by Catholic Supplies Ltd, New Zealand.

'Celtic Blessing', © Lesley K. Steel.

'Challenge the Normal', © Harold Williams, The Church of North India.

'Children of the Streets', Nkisheng Mphalele. Permission sought.

'Christ in Me, Christ in Others', © William Rutherford. Written during a Retreat on Celtic Spirituality in Corrymeela, Northern Ireland.

'Christ Our Advocate', © Kate McIlhagga from *Word in the World*, published by the National Christian Education Council (NCEC).

'Christian Love', Alexander Schmemann, *Turn to God*, © 1996 WCC Publications.

'Christian Toleration?', © Sue Brown.

'Circle', © Kate Compston.

'Circle Me', John Hunt, Christchurch, New Zealand.

'Come and Sit with the Carpenter', © Peter Trow.*

'Come, Great Spirit', © Norm S. D. Esdon.

'Come Holy Spirit', Evangeline Rajkumar.

'Come to the Living Stone', © Peter Trow.*

'Commitment to Creation', © Dr June Boyce -Tillman.**

'Compassion Is the Fulcrum', Andrew Pratt, © 1997 Stainer and Bell Ltd. Reproduced by permission from *Blinded by the Dazzle*.

'Compassionate Spirit', © Elizabeth S. Tapia.

'Conspiracy', used by permission of The United Church Publishing House; Margo Ritchie from *Images of Ourselves*, 1992.

'Contact', © Donald Hilton from *Flowing Streams*, published by National Christian Education Council (NCEC).**

'Contemporary Human Beings', Dumitru Staniloae, *Turn to God*, © 1996 WCC Publications.

'Conversion to Christo-centric Life', © The Indian Society for Promoting Christian Knowledge.

'Courage', an Indian proverb, author unknown.

'Creating Word, Living Word', © Jan Sutch Pickard. Published in *Vice Versa*, Church in the Market Place Publications, 1 St James Terrace, Buxton SK17 6HS UK.

'Creator God', John Hunt, Christchurch, New Zealand.

'Credo', by Dorothee Sölle from *Revolutionary Patience*. Published by Orbis Books, Maryknoll, NY. English translation copyright © 1977 by Orbis Books. Permission sought for use from Wolfgang Fietkau, Berlin, Germany.

'Creed of a Speech and Language Therapist', © Janet Lees, Senior Specialist Speech and Language Therapist, Epilepsy Research Team, Great Ormond Street Hospital for Children, NHS Trust, London UK.

'Dance and Sing', © Helen Richmond.

'Darning Spirit', © Silvie Purdie.

'Day's End', © Bruce D. Prewer from *More Australian Psalms*, Openbook Publishers, 205 Halifax Street, Adelaide, South Australia 5000.

'Destruction and Salvation', © Revd Dr C. M. Kao.

'Doctor with the Poor', Bishop B. D. Mondal.

'Don't Hide', Peter W. Millar.

'Dreaming in a New Reality', © Uniting Church in Australia, National Commission on Mission.

'Easter Reflections', © Elizabeth S. Tapia.

'Eat and Drink', John Hunt, Christchurch, New Zealand.

'Ecclesiastes Three', © Janet Lees, Senior Specialist Speech and Language Therapist, Epilepsy Research Team, Great Ormond Street Hospital for Children, NHS Trust, London UK.

'Enable Us To Be ...', Glenn Jetta Barclay.*

'Encounter at the Well', Cedar Duaybis from *Faith and the Intafada*, © Orbis Books 1992 Maryknoll NY.

'Enthusiasm for Life', Joanne Urtel.

'Eternal God', Masao Takenaka from *Your Will Be Done*, © 1984 Christian Conference of Asia.

'Evangelism', © Uniting Aboriginal and Islander Christian Congress, Uniting Church in Australia.

'Even the Stones Laugh', © Uniting Church in Australia, National Commission for Mission.

'Every Day', Shirley Erena Murray, © Hope Publishing Co/ CopyCare.

'Every Person Was Created', © 1995 Miriam Bennett.

'Exiles and Those of the Diaspora', © Daisy L. Machado. Used by permission, Carlos F Orlandi.

'Facing the Truth', © Uniting Church in Australia, National Commission for Mission.

'Faith', © Margot Arthurton.

'Faithful People', Tod Gobledale, Minister at Dombodema, Zimbabwe, United Congregational Church of Southern Africa.

'Fallen Angels', © Margot Arthurton.

'Fear', © Burma Issues.

'Fear Not', Dorothee Sölle from *Of War and Love*. Published by Orbis Books, Maryknoll, NY. English translation copyright © 1983 by Orbis Books. Permission sought for use from Rowohlt Taschenbuch Verlag, Reinbeck, Germany.

'Features', © Revd John Johansen-Berg.

'For Christ's Sake', © Rudolf Hinz.

'For Communion', © Janet Lees, an ordained minister of the United Reformed Church in the United Kingdom.

'For Music', © William Rutherford. Written during a Retreat on Celtic Spirituality in Corrymeela, Northern Ireland.

'For Our Land', Bishop B. D. Mondal.

'For You, Tourist', © Fepai F. S. Kolia. Originally in *Contours*. Permission sought.

'Forgive Us for Our Worship', © Duncan L. Tuck. Originally included in *Moods and Images*.

'Forgiveness', © Margaret Halsey. Written for Unemployment Sunday 1996 in South Yorkshire, UK.

'Free Treasure', © Duncan L. Tuck. Originally included in *Moods and Images*.

'From the Deep Recesses of Our Souls, We Cry Out ...', Sharon Rose Joy Ruiz-Duremdes.**

'From the Depths You Called', © Norm S. D. Esdon.

'Gentleness', © Derryn Best.

'Gethsemane Prayer', © Jan Sutch Pickard. Published in *Vice Versa*, Church in the Market Place Publications, 1 St James Terrace, Buxton SK17 6HS UK.

'Give Us a Voice', © Uniting Church in Australia, National Commission for Mission.

'Give Us Hope', Kim Kwan Suk from *Suffering and Hope*, © 1976 Christian Conference of Asia.

'Gleanings', Ana and Tod Gobledale, Ministers at Dombodema, Zimbabwe, United Congregational Church in Southern Africa.

'God Be with Those Who Explore': Michael Leunig's prayers are taken from *The Prayer Tree*. Copyright © Michael Leunig 1991. Used with permission of the publishers HarperCollins*Religious*, Melbourne, Australia.

'God Bless Our Contradictions': Michael Leunig's prayers are taken from *The Prayer Tree*. Copyright © Michael Leunig 1991. Used with permission of the publishers HarperCollins*Religious*, Melbourne, Australia.

'God Gathers', © Stephen Brown. * and **

'God Help Us if Our World Should Grow Dark': Michael Leunig's prayers are taken from *The Prayer Tree*. Copyright © Michael Leunig 1991. Used with permission of the publishers HarperCollins*Religious*, Melbourne, Australia.

'God Help Us To Rise Up': Michael Leunig's prayers are taken from *The Prayer Tree*. Copyright © Michael Leunig 1991. Used with permission of the publishers HarperCollins*Religious*, Melbourne, Australia.

'God in Hiding', Alan Gaunt. © 1997 Stainer and Bell Ltd. Reproduced by permission from *Always from Joy*.

'God Is Not Only Fatherly', from *Meditations with Mechtild of Magdeburg*, Sue Woodruff, © 1982 Bear & Co., Santa Fe.

'God of All Living', © Michael Durber published in *See, Judge, Act*, © Congregational Federation, Nottingham, UK.

'God of Good Ideas', © Janet Lees, an ordained minister of the United Reformed Church in the United Kingdom.

'God of Hope', used by permission of The United Church Publishing House; *There is a Season* by Betty Radford Turcott, 1996.

'God of Surprises', © Moira Rose.

'God of the Margins', © Jan Sutch Pickard. Published in *Vice Versa*, Church in the Market Place Publications, 1 St James Terrace, Buxton SK17 6HS UK.

'God of the Unexpected', Marjorie Dobson, © 1997 Stainer and Bell Ltd. Reproduced by permission from *Worship Live*.

'God Our Liberator', selected from 'The Hand of God' and 'Our Hands', © Kate Compston from *Word in the World*, published by the National Christian Education Council (NCEC).**

'God Our Reconciler', selected from 'The Hand of God' and 'Our Hands', © Kate Compston from *Word in the World*, published by the National Christian Education Council (NCEC).**

'God the Artist', © Dr June Boyce-Tillman.**

'God, Where Are You?' © Richard Becher.

'God, You Hold Me Like a Mother', Andrew Pratt, © 1995 Stainer and Bell Ltd and Methodist Church Division of Education and Youth. Reproduced by permission of Stainer and Bell Ltd from *Big Blue Planet*.

'God's Economy', © The Indian Society for Promoting Christian Knowledge.

'Good Friday', © Joy Cowley. Published by Catholic Supplies Ltd, New Zealand.

'Good News', © Stephen Brown. * and **

'Grain of Sand', © Margot Arthurton.

'Growth', © Joy Cowley. Published by Catholic Supplies Ltd, New Zealand.

'Guided in Silence by a Loving Hand', author unknown.

'He Was Laid in a Manger', © Goodwin Zainga.

'Healing Peace', John Hunt, Christchurch, New Zealand.

'Hear the Cry of the Weak', Andrew Pratt, © 1997 Stainer and Bell Ltd. Reproduced by permission from *Blinded by the Dazzle*.

'Help Us, Lord, To See You in the Dark Places', reproduced by kind permission of Trinity Hospice, Clapham, London, UK.

'Help Us To Think and Talk', © Brian Louis Pearce.*

'Hispanic Creed', © Justo Gonzales. Permission sought.

'Holy Saturday', © Peter Trow.*

'Home Coming', © Peter Trow.*

'Hope', author unknown, Haiti.

'Hospitality', © Joy Cowley. Published by Catholic Supplies Ltd, New Zealand.

'Houses of Hope', © Revd John Johansen-Berg.

'Humanity ... Inhumanity', © Margot Arthurton. Written for The Bosnian Arts Project, 1995 and sold to raise funds for Medical Aid in the former Yugoslavia.

'Hungry for ...', © Janet Lees, an ordained minister of the United Reformed Church in the United Kingdom.

'Hush! Take a Moment', © Silvie Purdie.

'I Am a Woman', © Elizabeth S. Tapia. First published in *No Longer Strangers; A resource for women and worship*, © 1983 World Council of Churches, Geneva, Switzerland.

'I Believe', © Janet Lees, an ordained minister of the United Reformed Church in the United Kingdom.

'I Believe in God', © Kate Compston.

'I Can Only Be Me', © Sylvie Purdie.

'I Cannot Become Identified', Austin Smith.**

'I Hear Your Sabbath Rest', © Norm S. D. Esdon.

'I Hold the Loving Cup', © Revd John Johansen-Berg.

'I Searched for You in Dusty Libraries', © Revd John Johansen-Berg.

'I Want To Live', The Friends of Chernobyl's Children Charity published in *Magnet*, Spring 1997, the quarterly Christian resource produced by the Women's Network of the Methodist Church, UK.

'I Weep', © Burma Issues.

'I'm Weary, Lord', © Uniting Church in Australia, National Commission for Mission.

'In a World of In-between', © Norm S. D. Esdon.

'In Affairs of Economics', Bernard Braley, © 1979 Stainer and Bell Ltd and Methodist Church Division of Education and Youth. Reproduced by permission of Stainer and Bell Ltd from *Worship and Where We Work*.

'In Constant Motion', © John Johansen-Berg.

'In Prayer', © Valerie Shedden.

'In Remembrance', © Kate Compston 1987 from *Encounters*, the Prayer Handbook for 1988 published by the United Reformed Church in the United Kingdom.

'In the End — a New Beginning', © Norm S. D. Esdon.

'In the Heart and in the World', © Eve Masterman.

'In Unexpected Places', Philip Andrews. Reprinted by permission of Uniting Education, PO Box 1245, Collingwood 3066 Australia

'Incarcerated', © Revd Ann Shepherdson.

'Intercession for the Homeless', John Sanderson.

'Interlocking Circles', © Kate McIlhagga.

'Invited Guests', © John Campbell, South Aston United Reformed Church, Birmingham B6 5ET UK.*

'Is There Any Hope?' Bishop B. D. Mondal.

'Isolated in My Grief', © Revd Ann Shepherdson.

'It Rained Most of the Night', © Brian Louis Pearce. From the story 'Not the Man from Notting Hill, published in *In London Clay* (Stride, 1991).*

'It's Not Easy, Lord', © Peter Trow.*

'Jesus Christ Is Waiting', from *Enemy of Apathy* (Wild Goose Publications, 1988), words by John L. Bell and Graham Maule, copyright © 1988 WGRG, Iona Community, 840 Govan Road, Glasgow G51 3UU, Scotland.

'Jesus Says', © Bruce D. Prewer from *More Australian Psalms*, Open-book Publishers, 205 Halifax Street, Adelaide, South Australia 5000.

'Jesus, Source of Life', arranged Ranto Ranaivoson.

'Jesus Stretched Out His Hand', © David Ya.

'Jesus the Compassionate One', © Aruna Gnanadason.

'Jesus Today', © Jill Denison.

'Journeying', © Revd John Johansen-Berg.

'Just the Way Things Were', John Sanderson.

'Leaving', © Marian Reid. First published in *Life and Work*, November 1996, the magazine of the Church of Scotland.

'Let My Work Live Again', © Norm S. D. Esdon.

'Liberating One', © Christian Conference of Asia.

'Life in Its Fullness', © Edward Cox.

'Like an Eagle', © Carys Humphreys.

'Litany of Commitment', prepared by the National Christian Council in Japan, Peace and Nuclear Issues Committee.

'Living Lord', © Brian Louis Pearce. From *Twickenham Prayers*, Twickenham United Reformed Church, UK, 1995.

'Living with AIDS', Frank Garoutte.

'Living with Contradiction', © Rupert Hambira.

'Lord, as Your Spirit Falls on Us', © Moira Rose.

'Lord, Liberate Us', © Revd John Johansen-Berg.

'Lord, We Know', from *The Rise of the Christian Conscience* by Jim Wallis. Used by permission of Sojourners, Washington.

'Lord, When Did We See You?', author unknown, from *Rapidas*, the magazine of the Movement for Latin American Evangelical Unity, Lima, Peru. English translation by WCC Publications, World Council of Churches, Geneva, Switzerland.

'Love Overcomes All', © Margot Arthurton. Written for The Bosnian Arts Project, 1995 and sold to raise funds for Medical Aid in the former Yugoslavia.

'Love Soars Where Eagles Cease To Fly', Andrew Pratt, © 1997 Stainer and Bell Ltd. Reproduced by permission from *Blinded by the Dazzle*.

'Loved by God', used by permission of The United Church Publishing House; *There is a Season* by Betty Radford Turcott, 1996.

'Loving Enemies', © Stephen Brown. * and **

'Make Us a Prejudiced People', © Stephen Brown. * and **

'Malagasy Hospitality', © Ranto Ranaivoson.

'May the Blessing of Light', source unknown.

'Messenger of Marvels', © Kate Compston.

'Modelled on Humour', © Duncan L. Tuck. Originally included in *Moods and Images*.

'Morning Tea', © William Rutherford. Written during a Retreat on Celtic Spirituality, Corrymeela, Northern Ireland.

'Mother Teresa and the Beggar Boy', Paul Sarker.

'Nativity', © Joy Cowley. Published by Catholic Supplies Ltd, New Zealand.

'Networking', © Dr June Boyce-Tillman.**

'New Wine under the Skin', © Duncan L. Tuck. Originally included in *Moods and Images*.

'No Harm Meant?', © Edward Cox.

' "Nobodies" to "Somebodies" ', reprinted with permission from *Pilgrims and Peacemakers* by Garth Hewitt, © 1995, published by The Bible Reading Fellowship.

'... Not Like Other People', © Jill Jenkins, 61 Lakeside Road, London N13 4PS UK.

'Not with Voices Only', © Alan Gaunt.

'Now!', © Carys Humphreys.

'O God, I'm Told I Must Compete', John Hunt, Christchurch, New Zealand.

'O God, She Came with Flowers', John Hunt, Christchurch, New Zealand.

'Older and Wiser', © Bruce D. Prewer from *More Australian Psalms*, Openbook Publishers, 205 Halifax Street, Adelaide, South Australia 5000.

'On the Wings of an Eagle', © Feiloaiga Taule'ale'ausumai.

'One Life', Kristone, © In God's Image.**

'Open Mind', Joy Cowley. Published by Catholic Supplies Ltd, New Zealand.

'Ordinary Folk', used by permission of The United Church Publishing House; *There Is a Season* by Betty Radford Turcott, 1996.

'Out of Silence', © Janet Lees, an ordained minister of the United Reformed Church in the United Kingdom.

'Outside the Church', Bart Baak.

'Palm Sunday', © Joy Cowley. Published by Catholic Supplies Ltd, New Zealand.

'Passover People', © John Campbell, South Aston United Reformed Church, Birmingham, B6 5ET UK.*

'Peace', taken from *The Universal Christ* by Bede Griffiths, published and copyright 1990 by Darton, Longman and Todd Ltd and used by permission of the publishers.

'Perceptive Soul', © Carys Humphreys.

'Peripheral People', © Stephen Brown. * and **

'Perspective', © Bruce D. Prewer from *More Australian Psalms*, Openbook Publishers, 205 Halifax Street, Adelaide, South Australia 5000.

'Pilgrim People', © Jill Jenkins, 61 Lakeside Road, London N13 4PS UK.

'Poor in Spirit', © Carys Humphreys.

'Prayer for Peace', author unknown.

'Prayer of Life', © The Indian Society for Promoting Christian Knowledge.

'Prayers of Touching', © Stephen Brown. * and **

'Praying for Shoes', © Richard Becher.

'Praying in the Market Place', Copyright © 1980 Sheila Cassidy, *Prayer for Pilgrims*, published by HarperCollins*Religious*. Used by permission of Sheil Land Associates Ltd.

'Someday Soon People Will ...', Norman Habel. Published in *In Unexpected Places* by HarperCollins*Publishers* Ltd.**

'Sometimes When We Pray', © Jill Jenkins, 61 Lakeside Road, London N13 4PS UK.

'Spiral of Life', used by permission of The United Church Publishing House; JoAnn Symonds from *Images of Ourselves*, 1992.

'Spirit of God', Lindsey Sanderson.

'Spirit of Life', © Prince Dibeela.

'Spirituality', © Bruce D. Prewer from *More Australian Psalms*, Openbook Publishers, 205 Halifax Sreet, Adelaide, South Australia 5000.

'Spring Cleaning', © Joy Cowley. Published by Catholic Supplies Ltd, New Zealand.

'Suffering Prayer', © Burma Issues.

'Take Our Hatreds', © Kate Compston. First used by Christian Aid.

'Teach Us', © Kate McIlhagga.

'The Busker', © Janet Lees, an ordained minister of the United Reformed Church in the United Kingdom.

'The Desert', author unknown.

'The Diary', used with the author's permission.

'The Everywhere Christ', © Richard Becher.

'The Face of Love', taken from *A Back Door to Heaven* by Lionel Blue, published and copyright 1979 by Darton, Longman and Todd Ltd and used by permission of the publishers.

'The Future Present', The Jewish Midrash from *Flowing Streams*, published by the National Christian Education Council (NCEC).**

'The Garden', © Richard Becher.

'The God Who Called Abraham', © Stephen Brown.* and **

'The Human Touch', © The Indian Society for Promoting Christian Knowledge.

'The Justice Tree', Shirley Erena Murray, © Hope Publishing Co./Copy Care.

'The Lesson', © Margot Arthurton.

'The Liturgy of the Tree', © Michael Durber.

'The Lost Dream', © Richard Becher.

'The Low Deep Sound', © Revd John Johansen-Berg.

'The No-childhood Child', © The Indian Society for Promoting Christian Knowledge.

'The Noise Nothing Makes', © Feiloaigioa Taule'ale'ausumai.

'The Open Doorway', © Jyoti Sabi, from a Christians Aware leaflet, 10 Springfield Road, Leicester, LE2 3BD UK.**

'The Path of Childhood', © Margot Arthurton. Written for The Bosnian Arts Project, 1995 and sold to raise funds for Medical Aid in the former Yugoslavia.

'The Silent Cry', © Harry Wiggett. Can be used or quoted in church magazines.

'The Silent Prisoner', © Harry Wiggett. As above.

'The Stranger', © Maureen Edwards.

'The Struggle To Be', © Prince Dibeela.

'The Two Brothers', Bart Baak.

'The Whole Creation', © Kate Compston from *Word in the World*, published by the National Christian Education Council (NCEC).**

'The Woman at the Well', © Kay Andrews.

'They Put Your Children Away', © Uniting Church in Australia, National Commission for Mission.

'This Is My Destiny', © Ranto Ranaivoson.

'This Is the Day', National Council of Churches India sub-unit on Youth, from *Your Will Be Done*, © 1984 Christian Conference of Asia.

'Those I Will Meet Today', © William Rutherford. Written during a Retreat on Celtic Spirituality, Corrymeela, Northern Ireland.

'To Be Fully Human', from *When the Heart Waits* by Sue Monk Kidd. Copyright © 1990 by Sue Monk Kidd. Reprinted by permission of HarperCollins*Publishers*, Inc.

'To Be Set Free', © Simone Rakotomavo.

'To Christ Our Creator', © Gwendoline Keevill.

'To Live Is To Go Around ... ', © Juan Marcus Rivera. Used by permission of Carlos F. Cardoza-Orlandi with permission sought from Christian Board of Publications Press.

'To See the Reality', © Raúl Fernández-Calienes.

'To the Poor Man', Economic Thoughts, Mahatma Gandhi, published in *Suffering and Hope*, © 1978 Christian Conference of Asia.

'Touching', John Hunt, Christchurch, New Zealand.

'Trash and Treasure', © Uniting Church in Australia, National Commission for Mission.

'Underneath the Arches', © Joan Gregory.

'Visual Prayer Ideas', © Jenny Spouge, 34 Dorrington Close, Luton, Bedfordshire LU3 1XR UK.

'Waiting for My Lord', © The Indian Society for Promoting Christian Knowledge.

'Walk Among Us Jesus', © Richard Becher.

'We Are ... ', © Richard Becher.

'We Are Caught in a Dragnet', © Revd John Johansen-Berg.

'We Are Going Home to Many Who Cannot Read', from *The World At One In Prayer* by Daniel J. Fleming. Copyright 1942 by Harper Row, Publishers Inc. Copyright renewed 1970. Reprinted by permission of HarperCollins*Publishers*, Inc.

'We Are Here, Lord', Action for World Development, Brisbane, Australia, from *Your Will Be Done* © 1984 Christian Conference of Asia.

'We Are Not Meant To Be ... ', © Bob Andrews.

'We Are the Church', used by permission of The United Church Publishing House; *There is a Season* by Betty Radford Turcott, 1996.

'We Came Together To Learn', © Revd John Johansen-Berg.

'We Have No King but Caesar', © Bob Commin c/o Mercer Books, 5 Roslyn Road, Rondebosch, Cape Town, South Africa.

'We Need Your Mother Love O God', words and music by Garth Hewitt, © Chain of Love Music 1993.

'We See Many Imprisoned ...', © Revd John Johansen-Berg.

'Weaver of the World', © Jan Sutch Pickard. Published in *Vice Versa*, Church in the Market Place Publications, 1 St James Terrace, Buxton SK17 6HS UK.

'Weaving', © Marjorie Dobson. Written for the Christian poetry contribution to the Bradford Festival 1994. Published in *Christian Poets from Yorkshire*, by Triumph House.

'Well-fed, Well-clothed', © Dorothea Sproule, Kensington United Reformed Church.

'Were We There?', © Marjorie Dobson.

'What a Joyful Celebration', © Revd John Johansen-Berg.

'What You Do to the Least', © Harold Williams, Church of North India.

'When Life's Crippled, Flawed or Faulted', Andrew Pratt, © 1991 Stainer and Bell Ltd. Reproduced by permission from *Hymns and Congregational Songs*.

'When Our Culture or Religion', Andrew Pratt, © 1992 Stainer and Bell Ltd. Reproduced by permission from *Hymns and Congregational Songs*.

'When Prophets Are Silent and Faith a Distortion', Andrew Pratt, © 1997 Stainer and Bell Ltd. Reproduced by permission from *Blinded by the Dazzle*.

'Where the Song Seeks the Singer', © Norm S. D. Esdon.

'Where You Are Bringing About Justice', © Juan Marcos Rivera. Used by permission of Carlos F. Cardoza-Orlandi with permission sought from Christian Board of Publications Press.

'Who Did You See?', © Richard Becher.

'Who Needs Words?', © Marjorie Dobson.

'Winter', © Joy Cowley.

'With Open Hands of Welcome, Lord', © Peter Trow.*

'Woman's Creed', © Alison Siu Moon Lee. 'Woman's Creed' is dedicated to 'All Christians who share and recognise the dignity of man and woman'.

'Words', © Maureen Edwards.

'World-wide', © Kate Compston 1987 from *Encounters*, the Prayer Handbook for 1988, published by the United Reformed Church in the United Kingdom.

'Yard Sale', © Sharon Backus.

'You Are the God of the Poor', © Batahola Choir via Carlos F. Cardoza-Orlandi.

'You Stoop To Fasten', © Revd John Johansen-Berg.

'You Teach Me To Listen, Jesus', © Revd John Johansen-Berg.

'You Were a Refugee Too', © Uniting Church in Australia, National Commission for Mission.

'Your Body', © Janet Lees, an ordained minister of the United Reformed Church in the United Kingdom.